EDUCATION

TEACHING METHOD FOR FIFTH GRADE

My Music Journal

FLORENTINA ALEXANDRU

APOLLO
PUBLISHING
www.mymusicjournal.org

PREFACE

Audio and video files can be found on our website **MyMusicJournal.org** and are publicly available examples intended for music education. All audio and video recordings are labeled per grade level. To access the recordings, go to MyMusicJournal.org, hover over the Courses tab, and then select the grade level. Please click the audio or video recording as it is labeled inside the music textbook. This website contains audio/video recordings created by Florentina Alexandru and external weblinks to audition classical pieces from famous composers. These recordings are intended to help students, teachers, and parents to follow along with the material in My Music Journal textbooks, such as practicing a rhythm, solfege, or learning to sing a song. For this reason, a parent or teacher must be present when a child accesses this material.

Standard Disclaimer for External Links

All external links are provided for convenience and informational purposes only. No external links found within the My Music Journal website constitute an endorsement or approval of any of the products, services, or content owned by the corporation, organization, or individual owners of these websites. My Music Journal is not responsible for the accuracy, legality, or content found at these external websites or subsequent links from these sites.

My Music Journal makes no guarantee that any material provided for download, viewing, or streaming on any external website is within the public domain in any specific country. Therefore, My Music Journal assumes no legal responsibility or liability for the copyright status of such materials.

Music Teachers

Please email us at mmj@mymusicjournal.org and request **Curriculum Outline and Assessments.**

Music Education: My Music Journal Teaching Method for Fifth Grade

Published in the United States by Apollo Publishing
5415 Lake Howell Rd. No 114
Winter Park, Florida 32789
United States of America
www.mymusicjournal.org

ISBN# 978-1-7339987-5-8
Printed in China

Table of Contents

Style (3 Lessons)

I am excited for the year ahead and can't wait to start writing

My Music Journal!

I look forward to learning how to play a musical instrument and even write my music. I want to explore the meaning of tempo, harmony, and pitch; learn about music composers, rhythm, dynamics, forms, genres, and texture to become a well-rounded musician. I have a feeling this year is going to be extra fun thanks to

My Music Journal!

Student Name: ______________________________

Dear students, parents, and teachers,

Music education is a continuous, systematic, and complex activity that begins in childhood and continues throughout your entire life. Did you ever ask what a life without music would be? Have you ever wondered how strange it would be to rock a baby without the famous "Lullaby," composed by Johannes Brahms?

What would it be like to dance without music—without body movement, without the accompaniment of musical instruments (drums, shakers, triangle, bells, recorder, etc.)?

Each piece of music—heard or read—brings new ideas and facts, which increase children's spiritual heritage and their ability to see, understand, feel, and appreciate. Children at very young ages demonstrate instinctual impulses to sing, regardless of their cultural environment.

Rhythm, for instance, is naturally expressed through breathing, walking, and most importantly, through our heartbeat. Human vocal cords are uniquely designed for a wide range of sounds, which helps express musical melody.

Music education is a necessary means through which students can discover and express their own emotions. Music classes provide students the opportunity to grow emotionally, mentally, and physically, as well as helping them with necessary life skills such as self-discipline, self-expression, responsibility, patience, and teamwork. Music education is a way to instill the love of music that will remain with students for the rest of their lives.

Pythagoras is widely known as the "Father of Mathematics" and the "Father of Geometry," but few know that he is also credited as "Father of Music" and the "Father of Harmonics." He discovered that musical intervals could be used for healing purposes and eventually became the first person to prescribe music as medicine. He applied the principles of harmonics to creative work—such as art and architecture—and extended them to multiple facets of life such as running a government, raising a family, friendship, and personal development.

Pythagoras taught that music could never be approached purely for the sake of entertainment. Rather, he saw music as an expression of "Harmonia," the divine concept that brings harmony to disorder and discord. Thus, music has a dual value, similar to mathematics, as it enables people to witness and comprehend various nature structures. Furthermore, he taught that if utilized properly, music can:

a) Bring harmony to faculties of the soul.
b) Compose and purify the mind.
c) Heal the physical body, thus restoring and maintaining perfect health.

Everyone, you included, has talent. All you need to do is allow it to shine.
Best of luck!

Florentina Alexandru

The Star-Spangled Banner

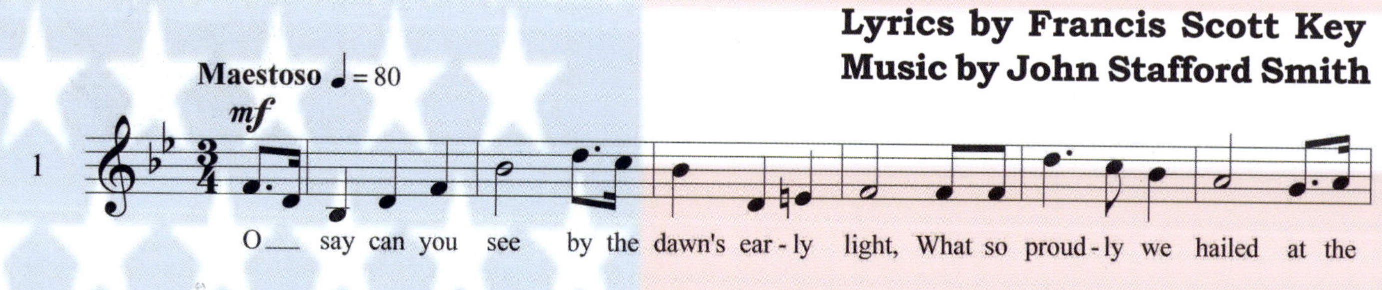

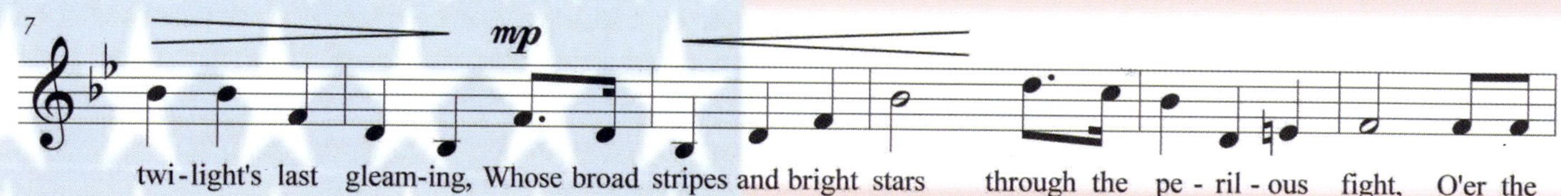

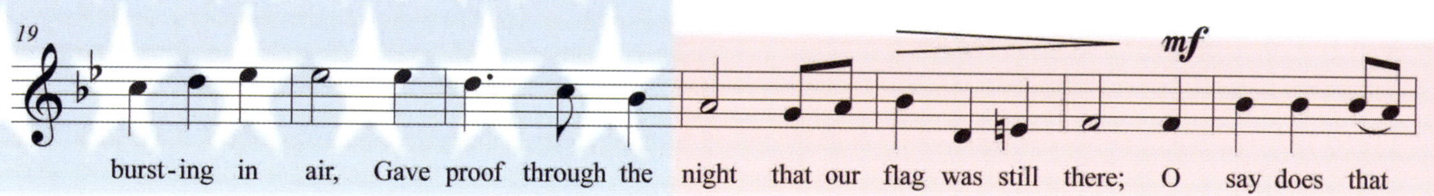

Oh, say can you see by the dawn's early light
What so proudly we hailed at the twilight's last gleaming?
Whose broad stripes and bright stars thru the perilous fight,
O'er the ramparts we watched were so gallantly streaming?
And the rocket's red glare, the bombs bursting in air,
Gave proof through the night that our flag was still there.
Oh, say does that star-spangled banner yet wave
O'er the land of the free and the home of the brave?

Audio F01

Listen quietly to "The Star-Spangled Banner."
Learn and sing the national anthem of the United States.

Swing Low, Sweet Chariot

Traditional Song

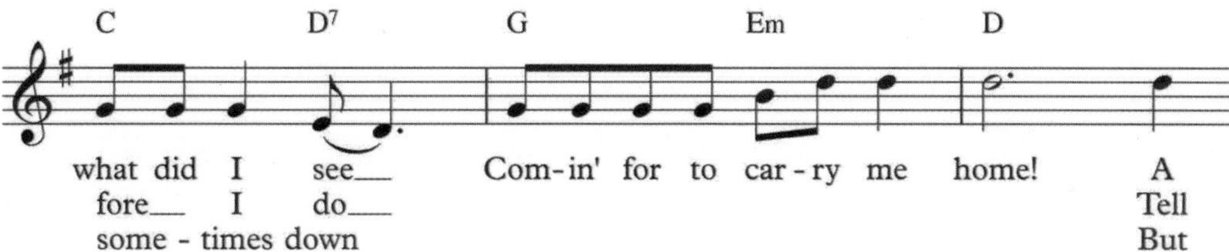

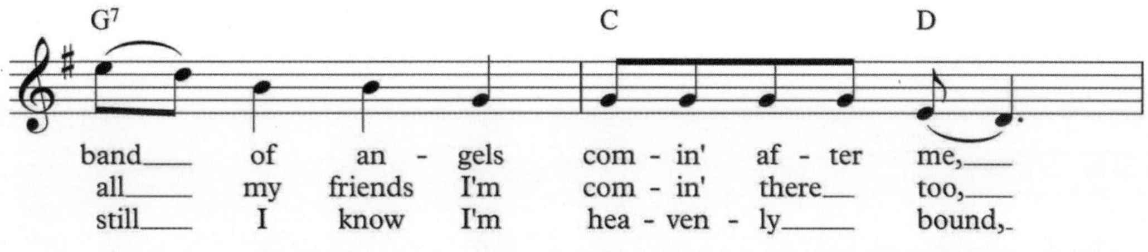

• It is important to devclop thc best voice because it is an integral part of your overall appearance. Effective verbal communication depends on what you say and heavily relies on how you say it.

• Sing the song correctly, with expressive, slightly rounded lips, clean emission, and loose body position.

• Sing clearly—refrain from slurring melody or stumbling over rhythm, hence maintaining proper posture while singing, with both feet on the floor.

Singing Voice

Take a normal breath and then exhale. Keep your shoulders low and chest relaxed. Repeat this exercise multiple times, ensuring that your breaths are focused in the abdomen region. Moreover, ensure that there is not associated chest, neck, or shoulder tension while breathing.

You can place one hand on your abdomen to remind yourself to keep the focus low and away from the chest and shoulders. Hold musical note "Sol" while you exhale.

Audio F03

Inhale
Inhale
Inhale
Inhale
Inhale
Sol
Exhale
Sol
Exhale
Sol
Exhale
Sol
Exhale
Sol
Exhale

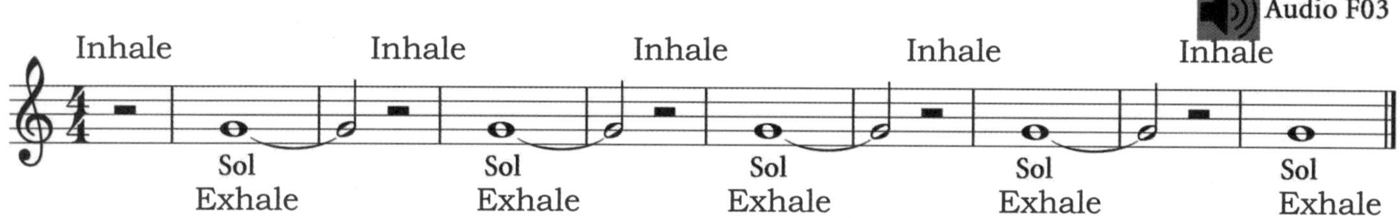

Let us work on our first exercise, which is to produce the "ssss, mmm, rrr" sound, while focusing on making the sound stable and keeping the volume constant.

Audio F04

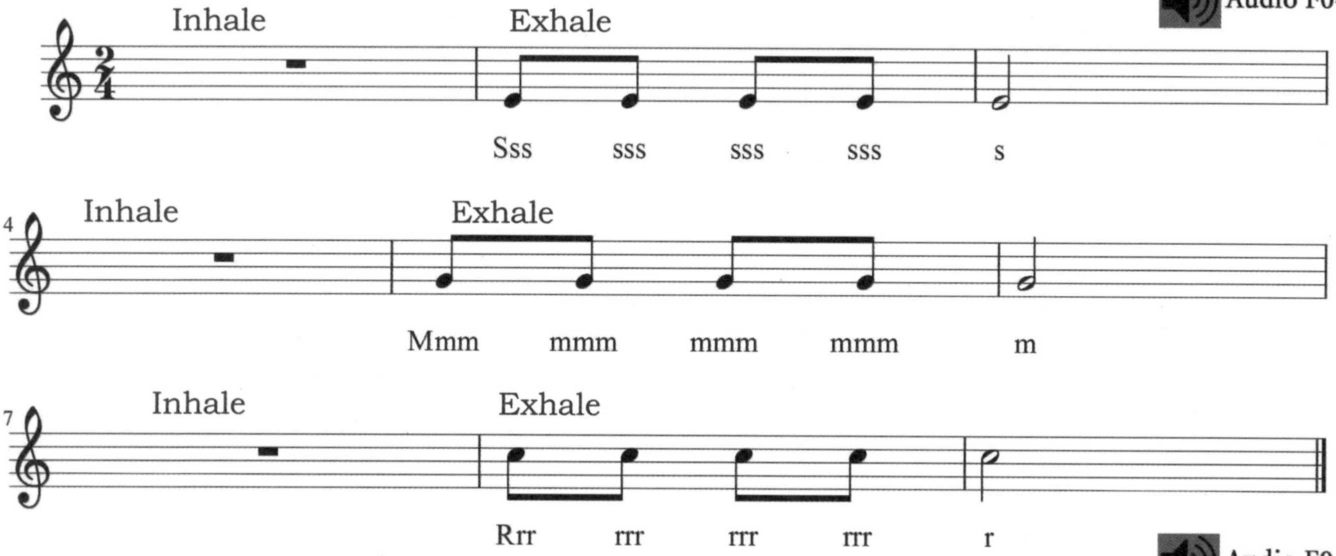

Inhale
Exhale
Sss sss sss sss s
Inhale
Exhale
Mmm mmm mmm mmm m
Inhale
Exhale
Rrr rrr rrr rrr r

Audio F05

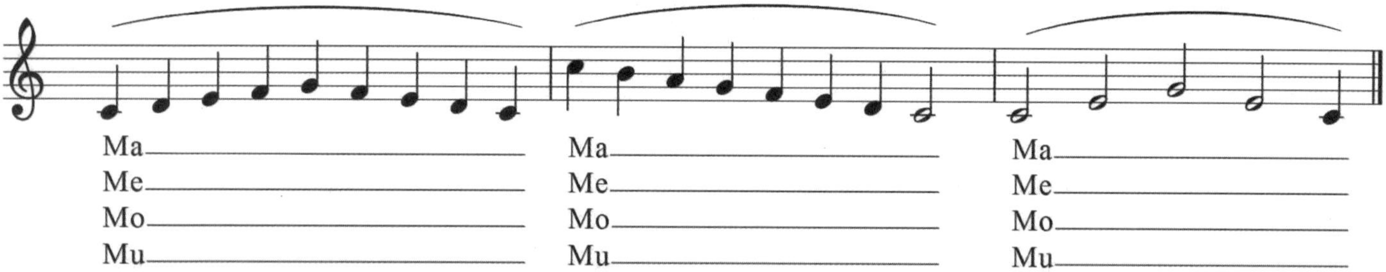

Ma
Me
Mo
Mu
Ma
Me
Mo
Mu
Ma
Me
Mo
Mu

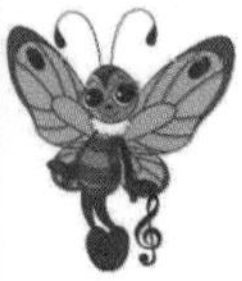

• Vocal warm-up improves the quality of sound and helps in preventing vocal injury; improves your voice, henceforth makes your voice production better.

• Take a normal breath and then exhale. Keep your shoulders low, and chest relaxed.

• Begin with released jaw and gently closed lips. Breath in and exhale while saying, "Ma__." Begin with the nasal sound /m/ and gently glide from high to a low pitch as if you were sighing.

The Ants Go Marching

• Take a normal breath and then exhale.

• Make sure your shoulders are relaxed and low.

• Place your lips loosely together, and release air in a steady stream to create a nice sound.

• Smile while you sing; this will help you develop a more clear and coherent sound.

• Have fun singing, "The Ants Go Marching."

Great Big House in New Orleans

Went down to the old mill stream
To fetch a pail of water,
Put one arm around my wife,
The other 'round my daughter.

Fare thee well my darling girl,
Fare thee well my daughter,
Fare thee well my darling girl
With the golden slippers on her.

- Sing the song correctly, with expressive slightly rounded lips, clean emission, and loose body position.
- Sing with emotion.
- Sing with a strong sense of forwarding motion—not allowing the word phrases to fade away, instead build them; sing with percussive consonants, as opposed to mushy pronunciations.

This warm-up exercise helps with:
- Intonation
- Breath control
- Tone quality

Time Signature 2/4

Although the terms meter and time signature apply to the same definition, they are used in slightly different ways. Meter is the property of music, based on an underlying, repeating beat rhythm, whereas time signatures are the symbols used to identify and describe the meter in a piece of music.

There are various time signatures used in music. Today we would be learning the 2/4-time signature.

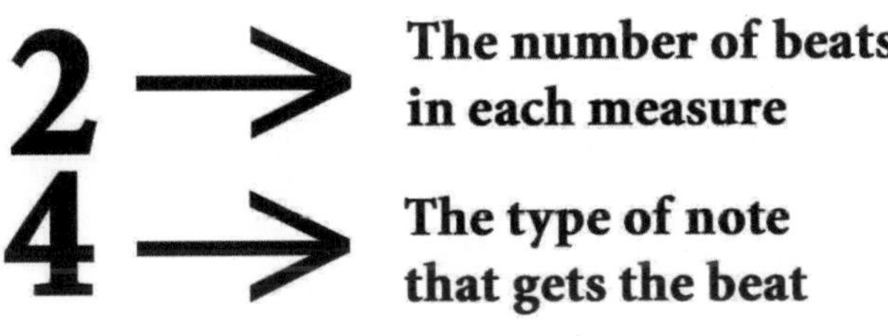

2 **There are two beats counts in every measure**

1/4 **The Quarter note gets the beat count**

The 2/4-time signature = 2 quarter notes per measure. In other words, there are two-quarter notes per measure. When measures contain two-beat groupings, musicians refer to the music as being in duple meter. It is important to feel the groupings of two and accent certain sounds accordingly.

The above sight-singing exercise will have a two-beat count-in because there is a 2/4 time signature at the beginning of the score. Since the smallest rhythmic value is an eighth note, you need to count 1 & 2 &. You must always strive to sing with the feel of the meter. Emphasize more on the first beat of each measure.

Goin' To Boston

Traditional Song

• Starting with 2/4, have the class sing “Goin’ To Boston” together while clapping the beat.

• Demonstrate the 2/4 conducting pattern, either by showing students a mirror image (conducting with your left hand) or by standing in front of the class, so the students can properly imitate.

• Students imitate.

• Class sings “Goin’ To Boston” together again while the teacher conducts along.

• Teacher sings alone while students conduct along.

• Ask for volunteers to conduct at the front of the class, using the special teacher’s baton, while everyone else sings.

Time Signature 3/4

The time signature describes the number and type of notes in each bar. In music, there are several different time signatures. We will be learning the 3/4 time signature today.

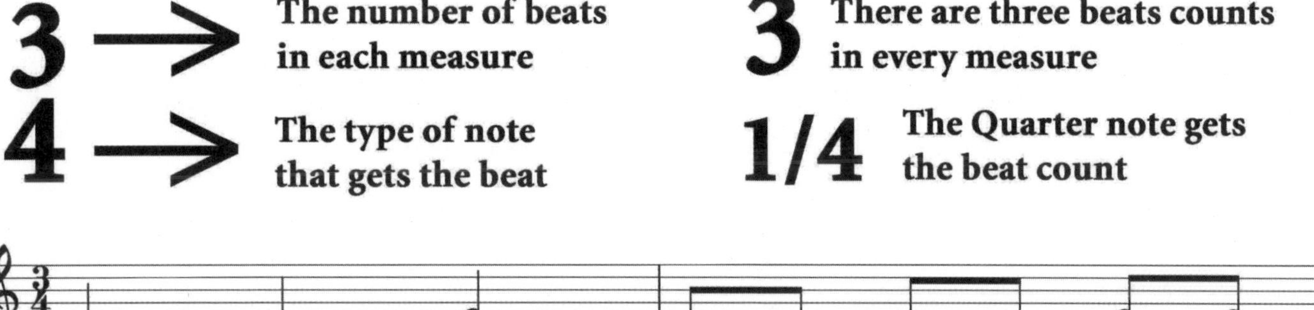

The 3/4-time signature = 3 x 1/4 notes per measure, or three-quarter notes per measure. When three-beat groupings appear in a measure, musicians refer to the music as being in triple meter. Allowing yourself to experience the groupings of three and accenting those sounds accordingly is very important.

Emphasize more on the first beat of each measure.
You must always strive to sing with the feel of the meter.

Silent Night

Audio F12

Traditional Song

C C

Si - lent night, Ho - ly night!
Si - lent night, Ho - ly night!
Si - lent night, Ho - ly night!

G7 C

All is calm, all is bright.
Shep - herds quake at the sight.
Son of God love's pure light.

F C

Round yon Vir - gin, Moth - er and Child.
Glo - ries stream___ from heav - en a - far.
Ra - diant beams from Thy Ho - ly face.

F C

Ho - ly in - fant so ten - der and mild,
Heav'n - ly hosts___ sing Al - le - lu - ia,
With the dawn of re - deem - ing grace,

G7 C

Sleep in heav - en - ly peace,___
Christ the Sav - ior is born!___
Je - sus Lord, at Thy birth.___

C G7 C

Sle - ep in heav - en - ly peace.___
Christ__ the Sav - ior is born.___
Je - sus Lord, at Thy birth.___

- Count the beats out loud (including the &).
- Keep going (do not worry if you make a mistake).
- Maintain your best singing posture.
- Sing with the feel of the meter.
- Have fun singing "Silent Night."
- Ask students to go home and think of songs that are in a 3/4-time signature.

Time Signature 4/4

Composers establish the number of beats per measure early on and then convey this information with a time signature. The time signature indicates the meter of a piece. The two numbers in the time signature inform us about the number of beats in each measure of the song. A song with a time signature of 4/4 has four quarter-note beats; each measure with a 3/4 meter has three quarter-note beats, and each measure of 2/4 time has two quarter-note beats.

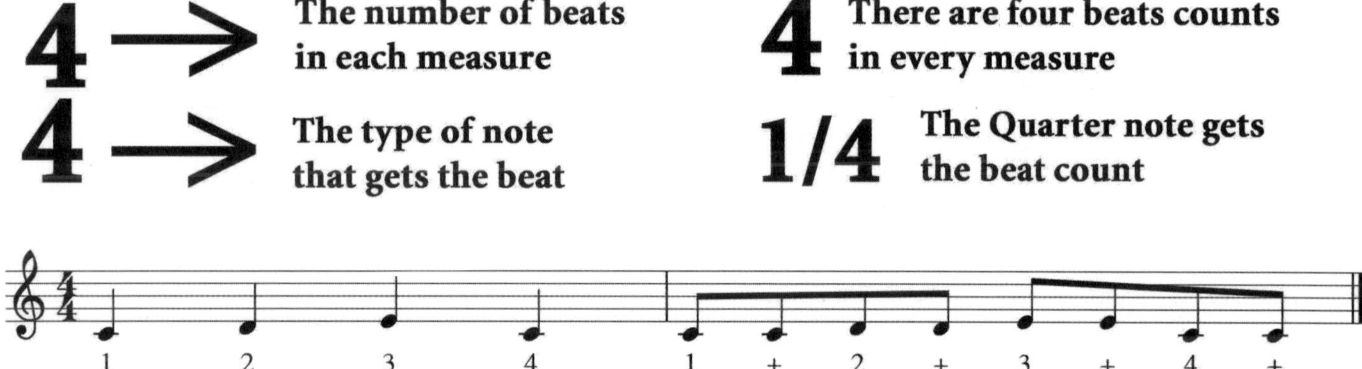

The 4/4-time signature = 4 x 1/4 notes per measure. In other words, there are four quarter notes per measure. When measures contain four-beat groupings, musicians refer to the music as being in quadruple meter. A time signature of 4/4 meter does not imply that each measure has only four quarter notes; in fact, it means each measure has only four beats.

These beats may contain half notes, quarter notes, eighth notes, rests, whatever the composer wants, but all note and rest values must be equivalent to the top number (or numerator) of the time signature.

You must always strive to sing with the feel of the meter. Emphasize more on the first beat of each measure.

Billy Boy

Audio F16

Traditional Song

• Starting with 4/4, have the class sing "Billy Boy" together while clapping the beat.

• Demonstrate the 4/4 conducting pattern, either by showing students a mirror image (conducting with your left hand) or by standing in front of the class, so all students can properly imitate.

• Students imitate.

• Class sings "Billy Boy" together again while the teacher conducts along.

• Teacher sings alone while students conduct along.

• Ask volunteers to conduct at the front of the class, using the special teacher's baton, while everyone else sings.

Time Signature 6/8

In previous lessons, we learned about the time signature. The time signature in the simple meter will have a 2, 3, or 4 for the top number. Beats in the simple meter can be divided into two notes, and beats in the compound meter can be divided into three notes. To have a better understanding, we will examine 6/8 time. The six eighth notes can be grouped into two beats (compound duple) or three beats (simple triple).

Since the simple triple pattern already belongs to 3/4 time, 6/8 is compound duple. Notice that each beat in 6/8 is a dotted quarter note. In fact, all compound meters will have some dotted notes, as it is a good practice.

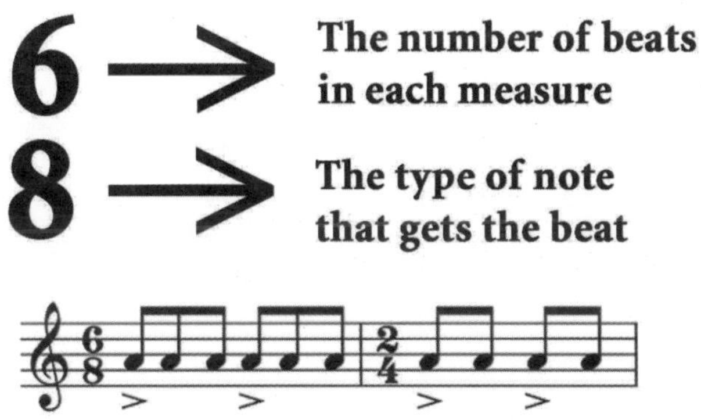

6 There are six beats counts in every measure

1/8 The Eighth note gets the beat count

6/8 time signature means count six eighth notes to each bar. This is a frequently used time signature. You can count the beats: 1, 2, 3, 4, 5, 6, 1, 2, 3, 4, 5, 6, and so on...

Did you notice that a time signature of 6/8 does not have a "4" in the bottom (denominator) position; you are no doubt already thinking that it cannot be a meter based on quarter notes. If you think that it might be a meter based on eighth notes, you are right. 6/8 time signature is a grouping of six eighth notes per measure.

You must always strive to sing with the feel of the meter. Emphasize more on the first beat of each measure.

Audio F18

Here We Go Looby Loo

Traditional Song

2. Here we go looby loo
Here we go looby light
Here we go looby loo
All on a Saturday night
You put your left hand in
You take your left hand out
You give your left hand a shake, shake, shake
And turn yourself about

3. Here we go looby loo
Here we go looby light
Here we go looby loo
All on a Saturday night
You put your left foot in
You take your left foot out
You give your left foot a shake, shake, shake
And turn yourself about

4. Here we go looby loo
Here we go looby light
Here we go looby loo
All on a Saturday night
You put your right foot in
You take your right foot out
You give your right foot a shake, shake,shake
And turn yourself about

5. Here we go looby loo
Here we go looby light
Here we go looby loo
All on a Saturday night
You put your whole self in
You take your whole self out
You give your whole self a shake, shake, shake
And turn yourself about

- Move to a steady beat.
- Distinguish between “long” and “short” duration of notes.
- Clap and echo rhythm patterns of the song.
- Tell children that you are going to sing a song that has numerous movement words. Gather children in a circle and ask them to hold hands. Demonstrate the motions by signing the song once in front of the class. Once the children have sung the song a few times, ask, what other ways can we move our feet? How does the song make you want to move your feet?

Movement Activity

Stomp the Rhythm

For each beat, you allocate a body percussion movement. You might stomp on quarter notes, slide on half notes, clap on eighth notes, and snap-on sixteenth notes, for example.

Then you do these body percussion movements while reading a piece of music.

Let's practice writing note values

Whole Note = 4 beats

Continue writing whole notes

Half Note = 2 beats

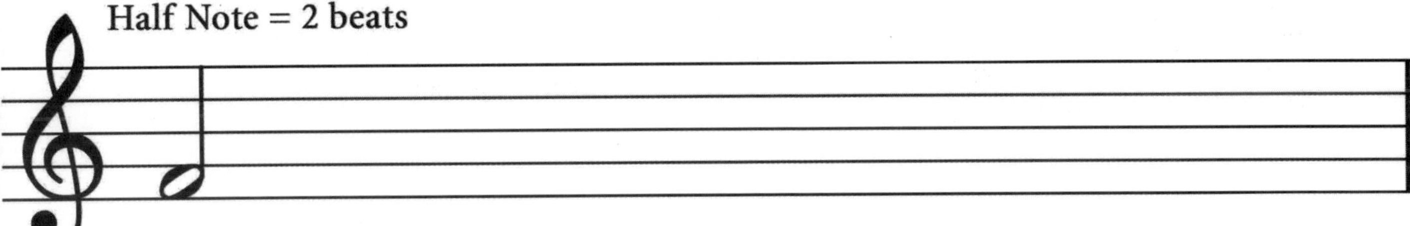

Continue writing half notes

Quarter note = 1 beat

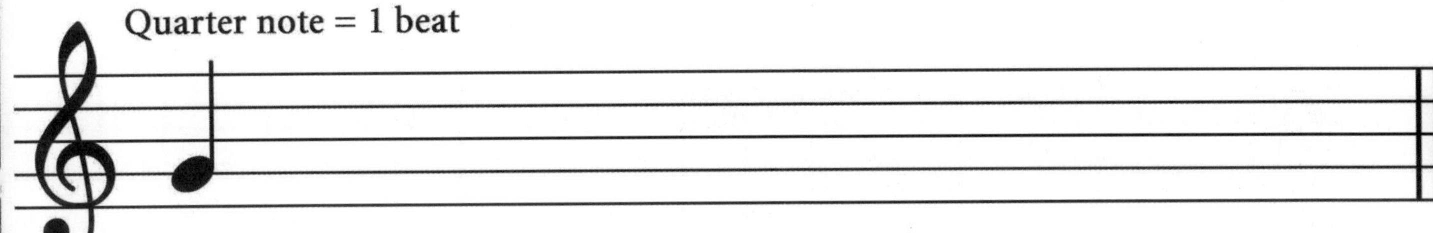

Continue writing quarter notes

Eighth note = 1/2 beat

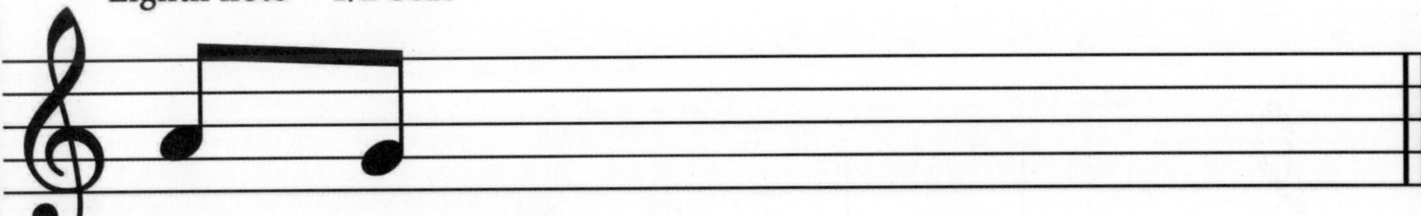

Continue writing eighth notes

Sixteenth note = 1/4 beat

Continue writing sixteenth notes

Name that musical note

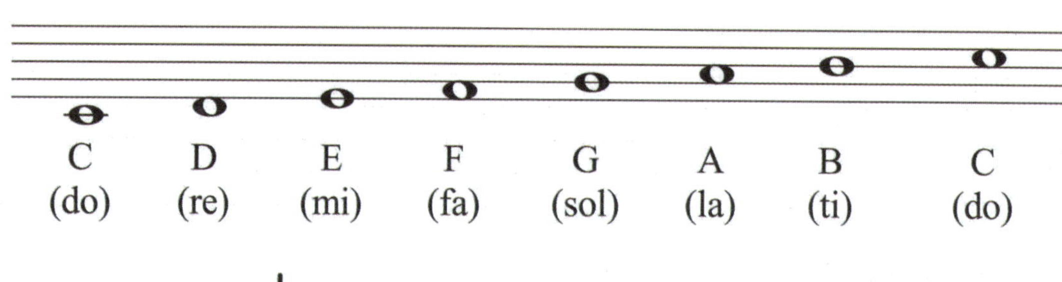

- Complete this worksheet by naming each note correctly.
- After you name the above pitches, echo sing, or sing as a group.
- Clap, tap, or chant the rhythm with metronome.

Audio F19

Let's compose a short melody and rhythm

Example:

Every measure must have two beats.

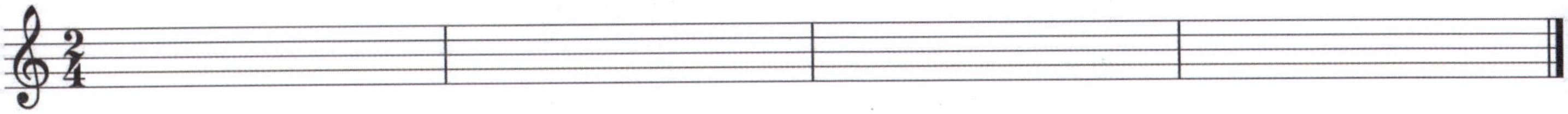

Example:

Every measure must have three beats.

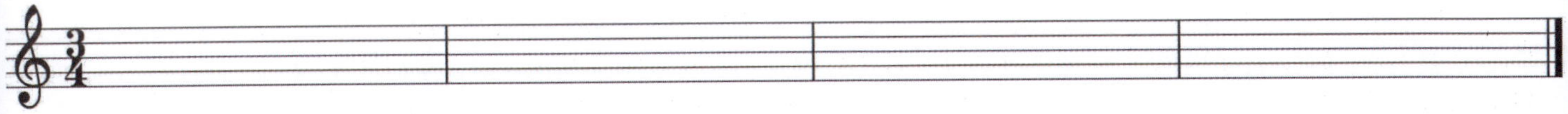

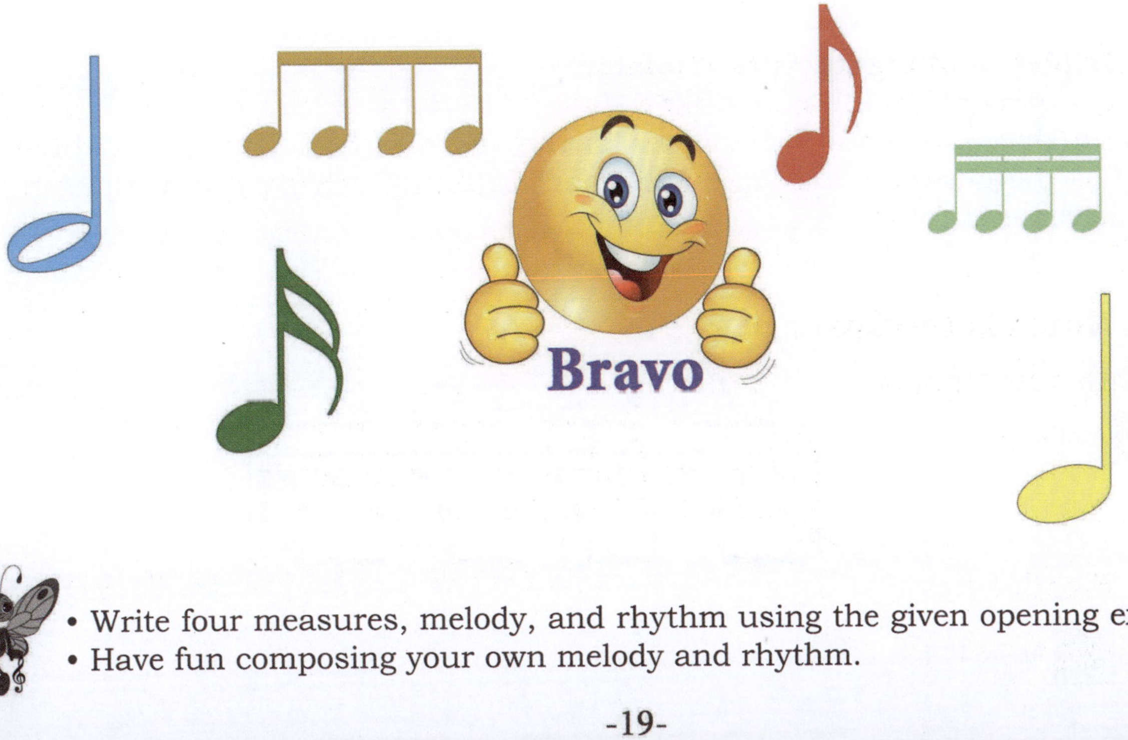

Bravo

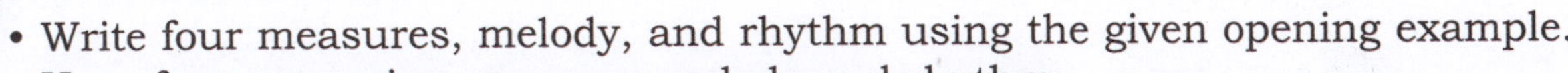

- Write four measures, melody, and rhythm using the given opening example.
- Have fun composing your own melody and rhythm.

Common time and Cut time

Common time, also known as 4/4 time, is a meter with four quarter-note beats per measure. It is often denoted as the common-time symbol: 𝄴

Cut time, also known as 2/2 or alla breve, is a meter with two half-note beats per measure. It is usually represented by the cut-time symbol: 𝄵

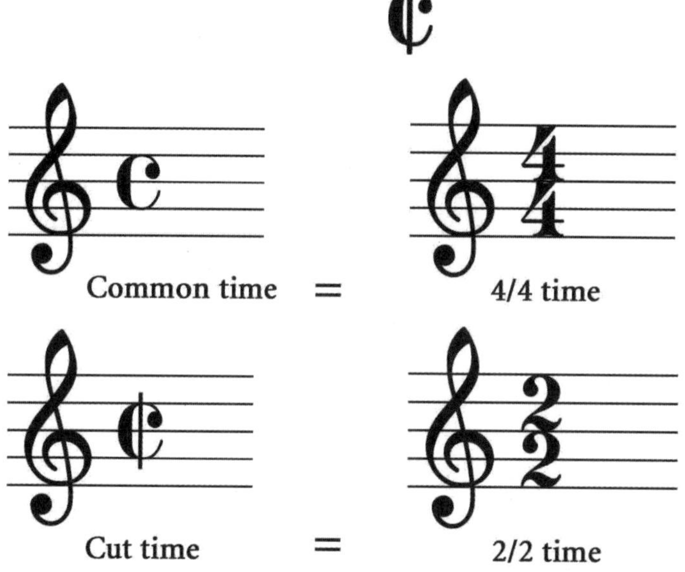

The Eighth Note Triplet Subdivision

A triplet is not simply the grouping of any three notes. Students often confuse it with three notes being played together, or if three notes are beamed together in written music. However, this is not necessarily the case. A triplet is a specific rhythm. A triplet is not a mere random grouping of notes.

What Are Triplets and Eighth Note Triplets?

Eighth notes compared to 8th note triplets.

A triplet is a rhythm playing three notes in the space of two. Triplet is a three-note pattern that fills the duration of a typical two-note pattern. Each note in a triplet has an equal rhythmic value.

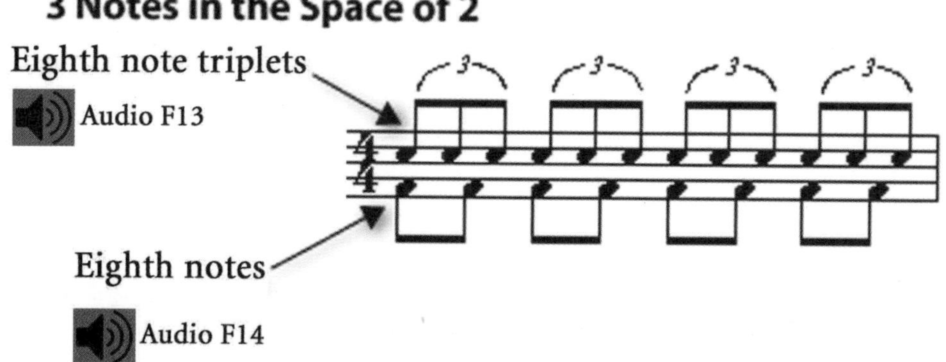

Solfege

- Review the concept of the beat, triplets, and have students clap the beat as they sing the solfege syllables.
- Instruct students to:
  - sing accurately and with good breath control.
  - relax and take a normal breath and then exhale.
  - keep shoulders low and relaxed.
  - place lips loosely together, and release air in a steady stream to create a nice sound.
- Practice the rhythm slowly, feeling three beats per measure.
- On this page, point out and circle the triplet rhythm.

Let's compose a short melody and rhythm

Example:

Every measure must have four beats.

Example:

Every measure must have six beats.

Bravo

- Write four measures, melody and rhythm using the given opening example.
- Have fun composing your melody and rhythm.

What is a syncopation in music?

When it comes to syncopation, expect the unexpected. Syncopated rhythms disrupt the flow by emphasizing a typically weak beat. This attention-grabbing and groove-inducing musical tactic is in use since the Middle Ages and still remains an essential part of current popular music. It is found in just about every genre.

In any given time signature, there are strong beats and weak beats. For example, in 4/4 time signature, beats one (the downbeat) and three are heavily emphasized traditionally, while two and four are comparatively weaker. On the flip side, in 6/8, beats one and four are the strongest. Syncopation is created when strong beats are obscured, and weak beats or smaller beat divisions are stressed upon instead.

Example of syncopation:

Audio F21

Two eighth notes tied together by a beam are equal to a quarter note. This rhythm is more commonly written as an eighth followed by a quarter note, which begins from the second half of the beat, followed by another eighth, as shown below.

Clap the following rhythm example of syncopation.

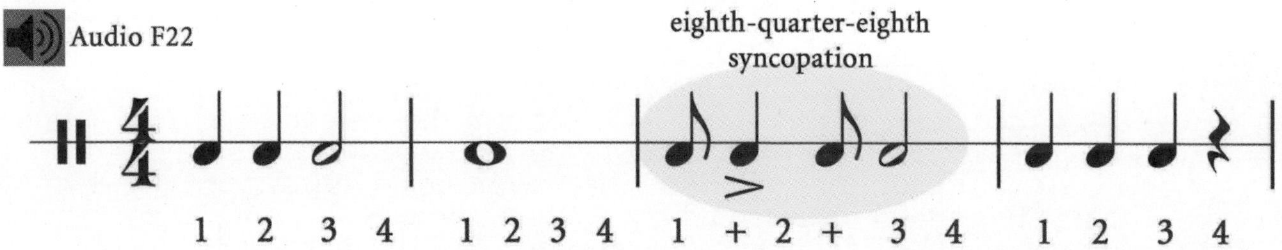

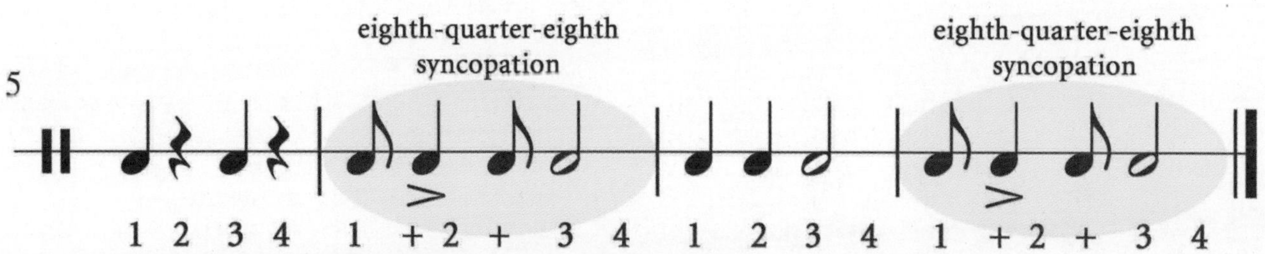

Try singing this rhythm exercise with syncopation. To help you hear and feel the rhythm better, emphasize the notes that have an accent mark ">" by the notehead (most of which will not be on the downbeat).

Run From The Farmer

Audio F23

Traditional Song

G G
Oh it's one gob-ble, two gob-bles, three gob - bles four, We will

C G
run from the far - mer for there's no time to snore.

G C
'Round and 'round we go, all 'round the coup,

D G
Run from the far - mer, do the loop - di - dee-loop.

Syncopation is a musical term for a jazzy rhythm. Introduce the song to the students as a chant first while working through it phrase by phrase. Write the syncopated rhythm on the board. Tell them, "I will clap the rhythm for you, and then I would like you to clap it back to me." Clap the rhythm. Check for understanding and accuracy. Repeat if necessary.

Tell your students, "This jazzy rhythm is played and sung several times during the course of this song. I will perform the song for you. Your job is to count the rhythm." They might need your help in understanding this concept, as instead of counting each note, they might be counting four-note rhythmic motive. Repeat the syncopated rhythm one more time before performing the song. Check for understanding and repeat if necessary.

Tell students, "I will play the song this time while you clap the rhythmic pattern each time you hear it in the song. You do not have to sing it this time." Check for understanding and repeat if necessary. Students clap the syncopated rhythm and sing at the same time.

Can you memorize this piece?

On this page, point out and circle the syncopated rhythm. Count the beats.

Movement Activity

Body Drumset

Show students a photo of a drum set for this activity. Discuss the various sounds produced by the drums. Then remind them that they will be using their bodies as drumsets.

You may need to locate a famous song's drum section.

Use your foot to get the lower drum, snare it with your legs, and place your hand on your chest for the hihat.

I strongly advise you to practice each drum part separately before attempting to play them together.

Then play it along with the music!

The Dotted Note

Continue writing dotted half notes

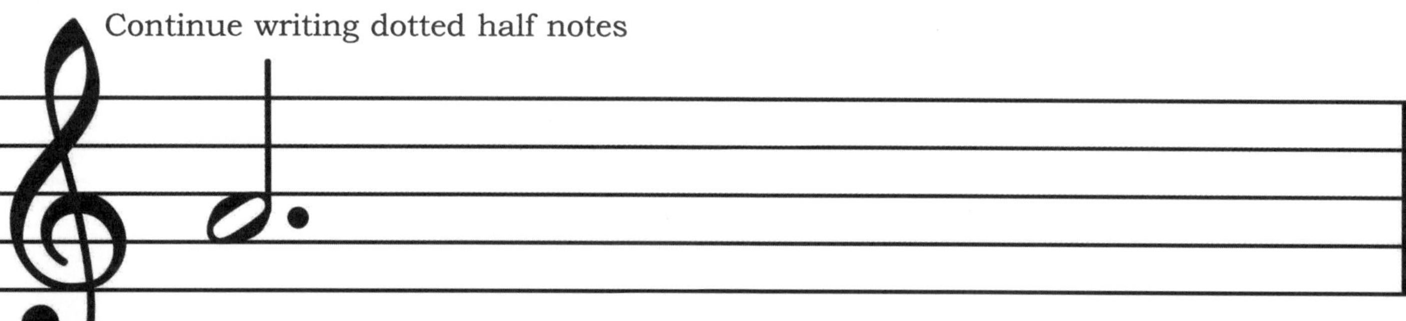

Continue writing dotted quarter notes

Continue writing dotted eighth notes

Note	Beats	Note	Beats
𝅝	4 beats	𝅝.	6 beats
𝅗𝅥	2 beats	𝅗𝅥.	3 beats
♩	1 beat	♩.	1½ beats
♪	½ beat	♪.	¾ beat

Dots are placed after noteheads to change the duration of a note. A dot adds half of the value of the note to itself.

For example, a dotted half note gets three beats - thc value of a half note is 2, half of 2 is 1, so 2 + 1 = 3.

Let us practice singing and clapping Dotted Notes

• Before singing these songs, take a moment of silent study to identify challenging rhythms.

• Write in the beat below each musical note, and the rest is indicated in both songs. Then clap the rhythm while counting the beats out loud.

Lil' Liza Jane

Audio F24

Three Blue Pigeons

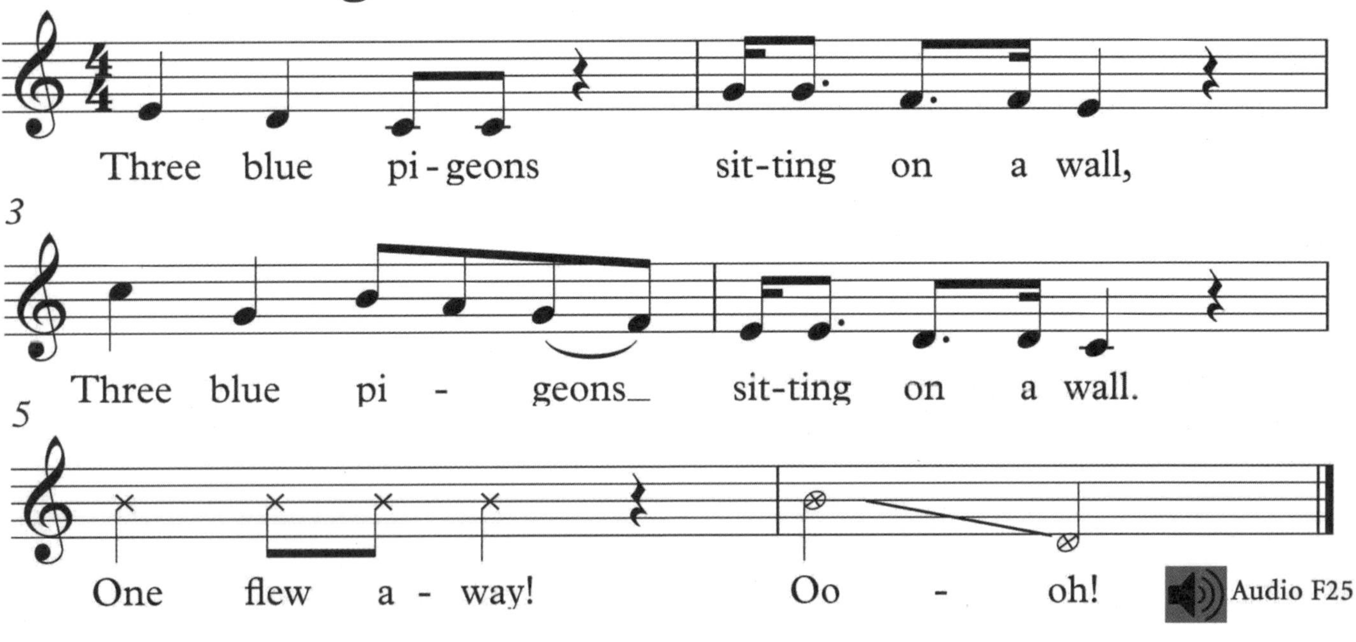

Rhythm exercise

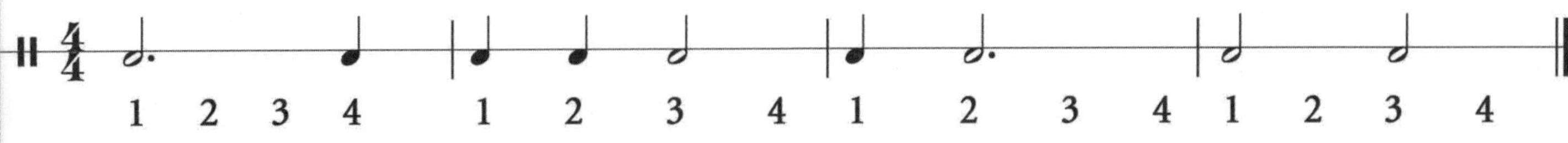

Audio F26

Music in the Renaissance

During the Renaissance, music was an essential part of civic, religious, and court life. In the period 1400–1600, the rich interchange of ideas in Europe, as well as political, economic, and religious events, led to major changes in composing styles, new musical genres, methods of disseminating music, and the development of musical instruments. In the early Renaissance the most important music was composed for church use.

A few characteristics of Renaissance music:

- Music based on modes
- Texture is richer and is in four or more parts
- Texture is blending rather than contrasting strands
- Harmony with a greater concern in the flow and chords progression
- Use of larger ensembles and demanded sets of instruments that would perfectly blend together across the entire vocal range.

Polyphony is one of the significant changes that mark the beginning of the Renaissance.

Thomas Morley

Thomas Morley (born 1557/1558, Norwich, England—died October 1602, London) was an English composer, singer, theorist, and organist of the Renaissance. He was one of the foremost members of the English Madrigal School. During his early years, he studied composition from William Byrd and took organ classes from Sebastian Westcote.

In 1588 Morley received a music bachelor's degree from Oxford and accepted the position of organist at St. Giles, Cripplegate. Morley has been considered the father of the English madrigal.

Famous madrigals by Morley include *Aprill is in my mistris face, My bonny lasse shee smyleth, Now is the month of maying, O sleep, fond fancy, Sing wee and chaunt it, Sweet nymphe, come to thy lover,* and *Though Philomela lost her love.* Solo songs by Morley include, *It was a lover and his lasse*, a song which also appears in Shakespeare's pastoral comedy, *As You Like It.*

Coloring Time...Fun...Fun

Thomas Morley

Audio F27

While coloring, you may listen to *Pavane,* composed by Thomas Morley.

Thomas Morley Quiz

1. Who was Thomas Morley's important and influential teacher?
a) William Byrd
b) William Billings
c) Orlando Gibbons
d) Orlando de Lassus

2. In 1588 Morley received a Bachelor of Music degree from _____________.
a) Paris
b) Oxford
c) Venice

3. Morley has been called the father of the English _______________________.
a) Sonata
b) Madrigal
c) Symphony

4. This madrigal by Thomas Morley is used in Shakespeare's play, *As You Like It* (the refrain ends with *Sweet lovers love the spring*).
a) Now is the Month of Maying
b) April is in my Mistress' Face
c) It was a Lover and His Lasse
d) My Bonny Lass, She Smileth

Folklore and Music of Romania

Folk music is Romania's oldest mode of musical expression. It is characterized by great vitality. Romanian folk music is the defining source of cultured musical creation. Conservation of Romanian folk music was aided by a large and enduring audience and by numerous performers who helped propagate and further develop folk music. One of them is Gheorghe Zamfir. He is very famous throughout the world. Gheorghe Zamfir helped in popularizing the traditional Romanian folk instrument, the panpipes.

The religious musical creation, developed under Byzantine music's influence and modified to the local folk music intonations, saw a period of glory between the 15th-17th centuries. In Romanian Monasteries were established reputed schools of liturgical music.

Gheorghe Zamfir

Romanian Folk Group

Doina is a lyrical, instrumental, or vocal creation specific to the Romanian people. The unknown author directly expresses his feelings of mourning, alienation, revolt, sadness, love, hatred against oppressors, regret, etc.

The *Doina* is a free-rhythmic, strongly ornamented (usually melismatic), improvised tune. The improvisation is performed on a more or less predetermined pattern (usually descending) by extending the notes in a rubato-like manner, depending on the performer's mood and imagination. The prolonged notes are usually the fourth or fifth above the floor note. The peasant *Doinas* are mainly vocal and monophonic, with some vocal peculiarities that differ by location: interjections (mai, hei, dui-dui, iuhu), glottal clucking sounds, choked sobbing effects, and so on. Instrumental *Doinas* are played on basic instruments, usually flutes or even primitive ones like a leaf. The peasant *Doina* is a non-ceremonial form of song that is usually sung in solitude, with a significant psychological effect: to "ease one's soul."

Until 1900, *Doina* was the only musical genre in many regions of the country. Sometimes *Doina* is sung with some vocal peculiarities like interjections, glottal clucking sounds, choked sobbing effects, etc., which vary from place to place. Instrumental *Doina* is played on simple instruments, like flutes, or even on rudimentary ones, such as a leaf. In 2009, *Doina* was included in the UNESCO list of Intangible Cultural Heritage.

You may listen to *Ciocarlia (F28), The Lonely Shepherd* (F29) played by Gheorghe Zamfir and *Doina din Maramures* by Maria Tanase.

Audio F28, F29, F29a

Musical Instruments Puzzle

Find and circle the words in this puzzle

T	R	O	M	B	O	N	E	O	O	T	S	T	N
T	B	R	A	V	O	B	E	F	E	Z	N	R	A
E	T	A	N	I	E	L	A	C	A	R	I	E	E
N	R	T	I	O	R	E	O	G	B	E	D	D	C
R	N	I	R	L	A	A	L	C	P	R	N	R	E
O	O	U	A	A	N	L	F	D	C	I	O	O	P
C	R	G	C	H	S	F	N	L	D	I	P	C	I
S	A	X	O	P	H	O	N	E	U	I	P	E	P
N	N	O	I	D	R	O	C	C	A	T	F	R	N
O	H	A	R	M	O	N	I	C	A	C	E	S	A
R	T	T	E	P	M	U	R	T	D	E	O	E	P
N	I	A	O	B	A	Z	O	O	K	A	B	P	O
R	E	H	T	I	Z	T	D	T	G	U	O	P	S
N	C	C	L	A	R	I	N	E	T	P	E	I	C

FLUTE
HARMONICA
RECORDER
OBOE
TROMBONE
GUITAR
VIOLA
CORNET
SAXOPHONE
BAZOOKA
ACCORDION
TRUMPET
PAN PIPE
CLARINET
BAGPIPE
ZITHER
PICCOLO
OCARINA
FIDDLE
SNARE

Sharp, Flat, and Natural Notes

A note's pitch describes how high or lows the sound is. Pitch is determined by the frequency of the note's fundamental sound wave. The higher a sound wave's frequency, the shorter its wavelength and the higher its pitch. However, musicians usually don't like to talk about wavelengths and frequencies. Instead, they refer to them as different letters: A, B, C, D, E, F, and G. These seven letters are all-natural notes within one octave (on a keyboard, that is all the white keys). (When you reach the eighth natural note, begin the next octave with another A.)

While the role of the sharp is to raise a note by a semitone, and the flat is to lower a note by a semitone, the natural, on the other hand, "cancels" the previous sharp or flat. It lowers a sharpened note by a semitone or raises a flattened note by a semitone.

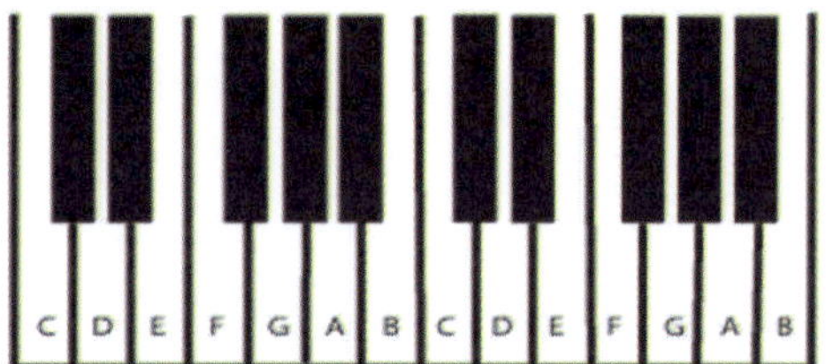

However, in Western music each octave commonly uses twelve notes. How do you name the other five notes (on a keyboard, the black keys)?

The sharp symbol (#) placed before a note notifies you to play the very next note up. The very next note up may either be a black or white key. Here "G" is "G sharp," and you play the very next note up on the keyboard.

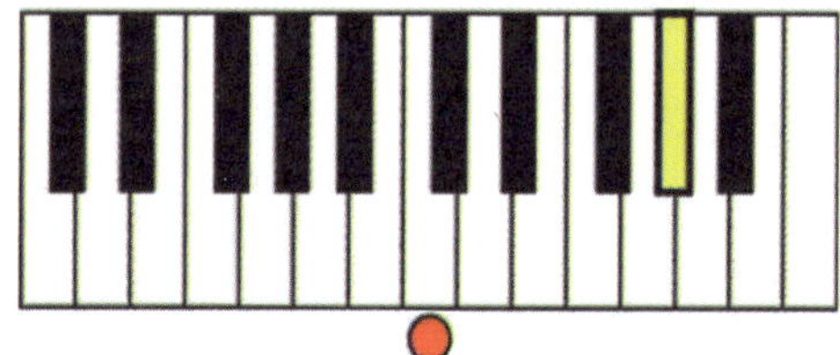

A flat symbol (♭)placed before a musical note tells you to play the very next note down. The very next note down may either be a black or white key. Here "G" is "G flat," and you play the very next note down on the keyboard.

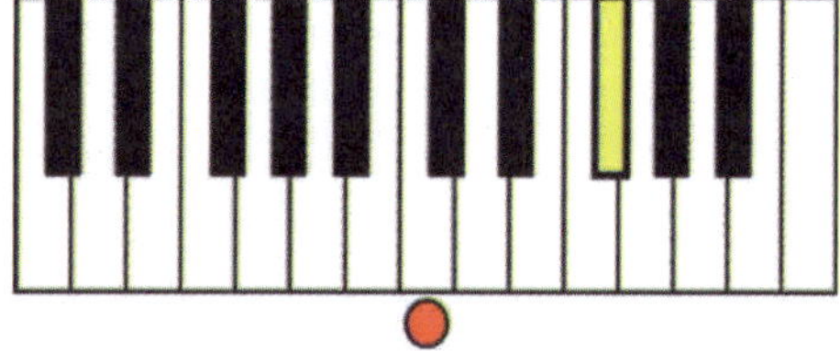

A natural symbol (♮) cancels any prior sharps or flats for that particular note, including any sharps or flats in the key signature.

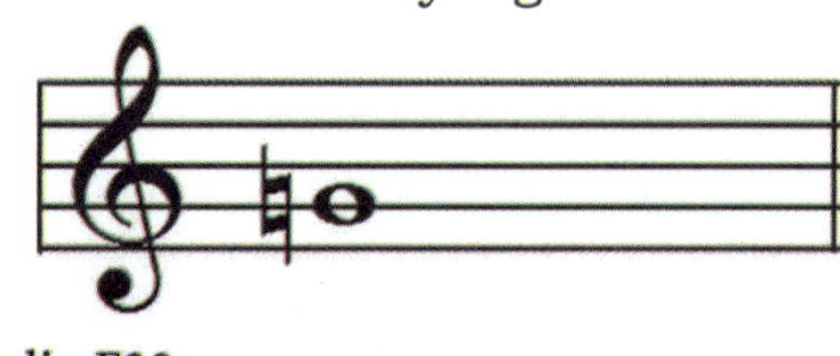

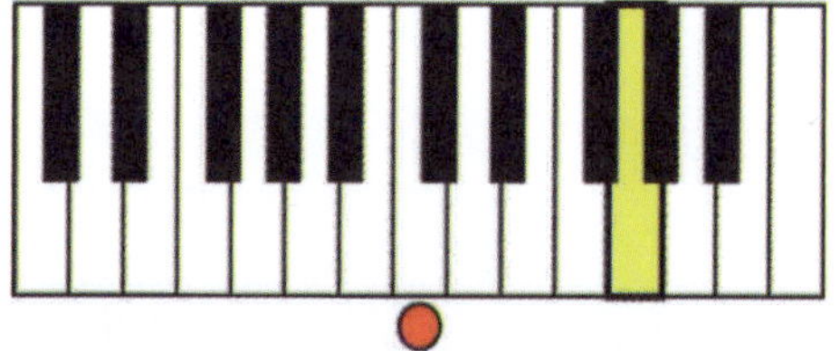

Audio F30

Solfege

Audio F31

- Sing with accurate pitch and proper tuning.
- Can you recognize the sharps, flats, and naturals and the changes in pitch?
- Take this slowly and really concentrate on how each note sounds.
- In each measure, we have four beats. Sing a bit louder first solfege syllable of the first beat.
- On this page point out, and circle the dotted half note.

Accidental Review

Sharp Flat Natural

Draw 3 sharp symbols in the box below

Draw 3 flat symbols in the box below

Draw 3 natural symbols in the box below

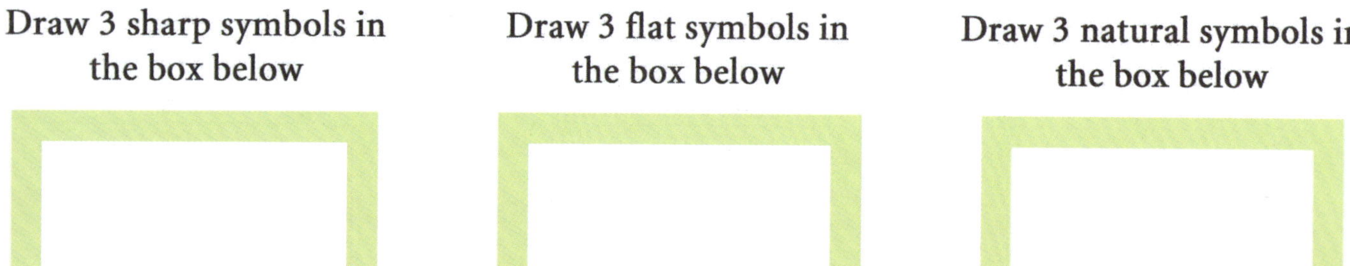

Add accidentals to complete each note below. Be sure to carefully place them on the line or in the space in front of the proper note.

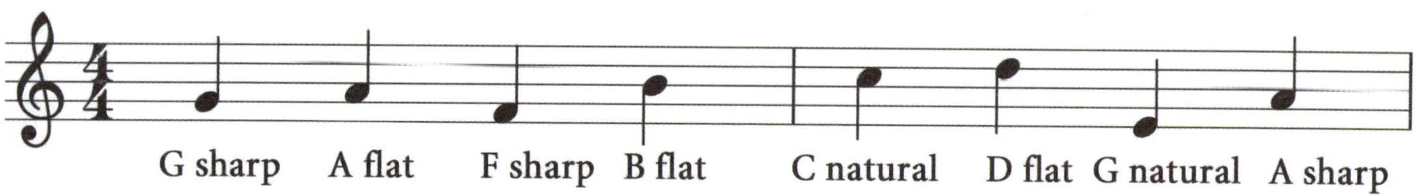

Let's have fun learning piano

Today we will be learning to play C major scale, C minor scale, and the Chromatic scale. Minor scales sound different from major scales because they are based on a different pattern of intervals. In music, a scale is a succession of pitches ascending or descending in steps that are related to the same key. Each scale begins on its keynote (also called the tonic), which matches the name of the scale. For instance, if you are going to play a C major scale, you'll begin on the note C.

C major scale has the following notes: C, D, E, F, G, A, B, C. When you start to play the scale, the first note is usually repeated at the end, one octave higher. In this case, that's the note C. The C major scale is the most comfortable piano scale to learn first since it uses only white keys on the piano.

There are a few "black notes" between some pairs, but not between all. There are two steps between C and D because there is a black note between them; similarly, D to E is also two steps, however from E to F is one step because there is no black note between them; F to G, G to A and A to B are all two steps, but B to C is one step. These steps are called half tones, and there are in total 12 of them in an octave.

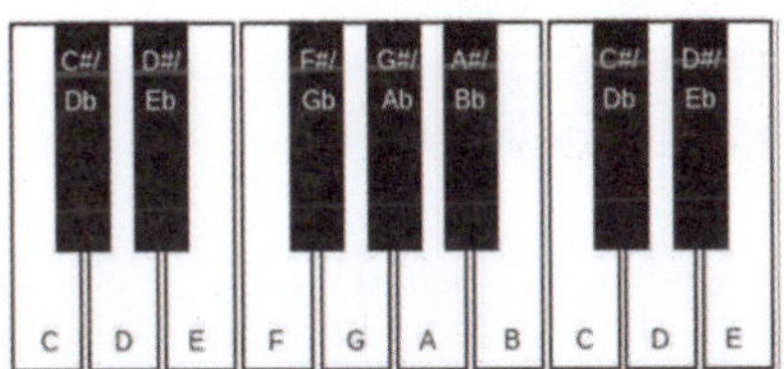

Pick two consecutive white musical notes on the keyboard, which have a black note in between, play the two white notes. Then try playing the black note in between.

Try singing and playing a "chromatic" scale – that is, all the notes, white and black in ascending and descending order.

The difference between major and minor is usually the difference in moods. Major scales often induce feelings of happiness and joy. Minor scales are definitely more somber and have a tendency to dampen one's spirits.

C Major Scale

Play C major scale, C minor scale, and the Chromatic scale on the piano.

Please view Video L25.

Video L25

All major scales share the same pattern: Whole-Whole-Half-Whole Whole-Whole-Half. For example, a C major scale would be C-D-E-F-G-A-B-C.

C Minor Scale

Minor scales follow a similar structure: Whole-Half-Whole-Whole-Half-Whole-Whole. For example, a C minor scale would be C-D-E♭-F-G-A♭-B♭-C

Half Steps and Whole Steps

The half step (H) or semitone is the smallest interval used in traditional Western music. On a piano keyboard, a half step is represented by two adjacent keys. The whole step (W) is an interval made by combining two half steps.

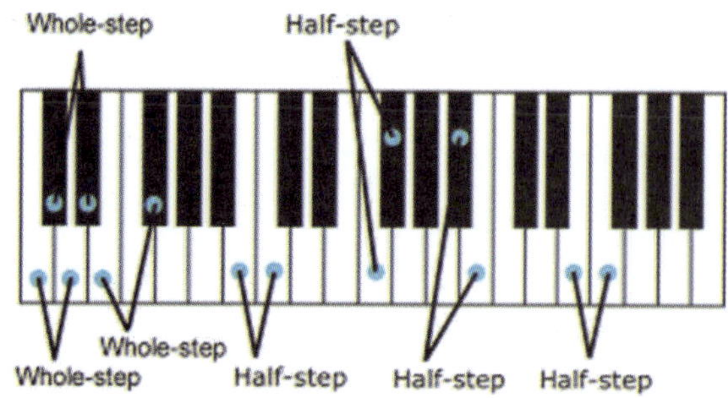

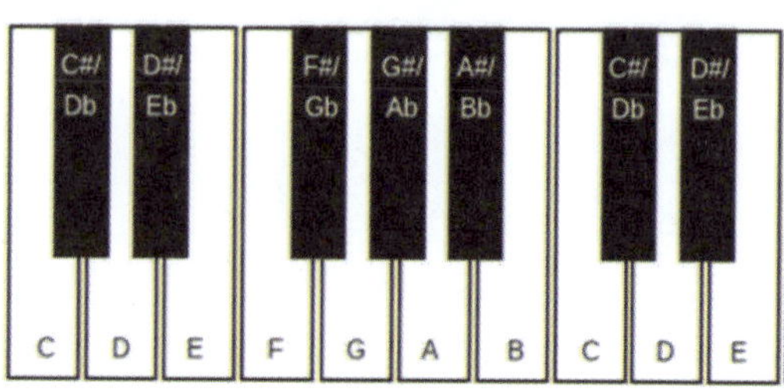

On the line beneath each piano keyboard image, write whether the interval indicated by the O's is a half step (H) or whole step (W).

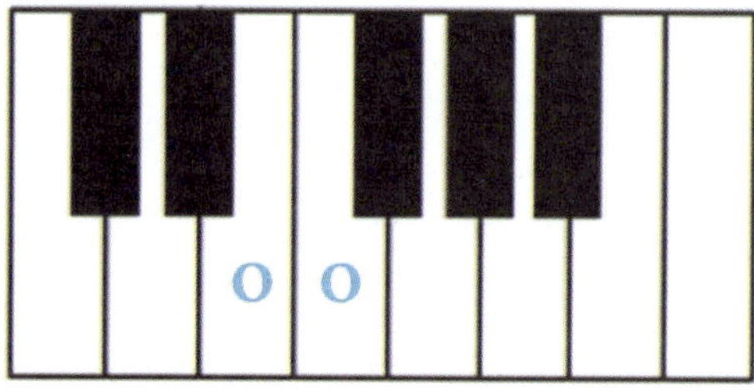

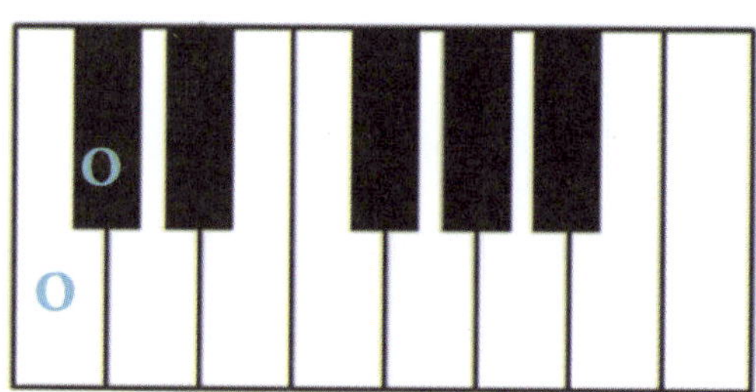

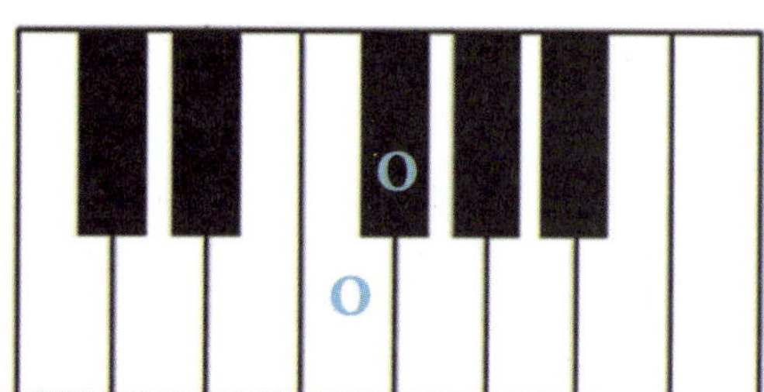

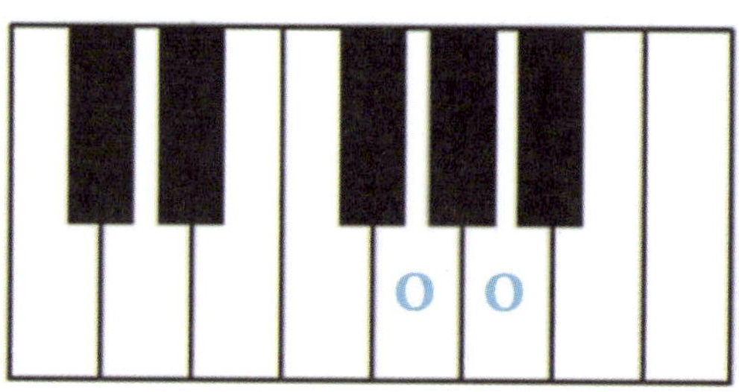

Write on the line, whether the pair of notes represents a half step (H) or whole step (W).

Mama Paquita

Traditional Song

Ma-ma Pa - qui- ta! Ma-ma Pa - qui- ta! Ma-ma Pa - qui - ta buy your ba-by a pa-
qui- ta! Ma-ma Pa - qui- ta! Ma-ma Pa - qui - ta buy your ba-by some pa-

pay - a, a ripe pa - pay - a, and a ba - na - na, a ripe ba -
jam - as, some nice pa - jam - as, a yel-low blank-et, a yel-low

C Major Scale

Audio F33

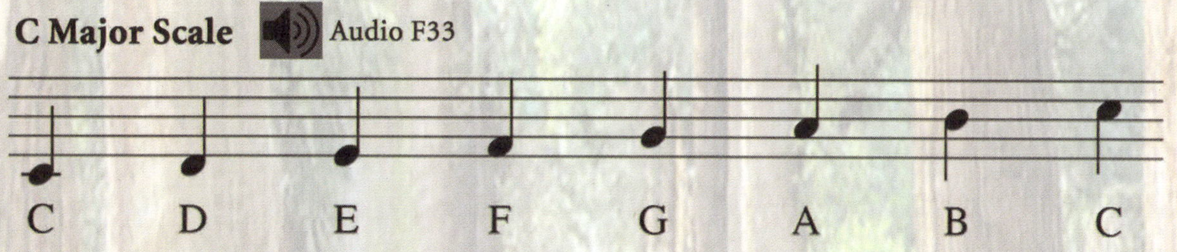

Singing musical scales (for example, C major scale) is a great way to warm-up our voices. Singing scales are extremely useful to keep us in pitch when we sing! Singing scales improve pitch memory (the ability to hear notes and phrases and accurately sing those notes and phrases), which is essential for the singer's ear training. Practicing scales expand the vocal range. For example, you can choose whether to sing a scale (ascending, descending, or both methods combined) on vowels or solfege syllables.

After you warm-up, your voices on C major scale sing "Mama Paquita" song. "Mama Paquita" is written in C major. Does this song sound happy or sad? Did you notice the repeat sign alongside the first and second ending? What else do you notice in this song?

Can you find a dance movement while listening to this song?

With your partner, analyze and talk about note values, 1st and 2nd ending, count the beats, number the measures, circle the quarter rests.

Describe what you like the most about this piece, rhythm, melody, lyrics, etc.

Minor Tonality

All The Pretty Little Horses

Audio F34

Traditional Song

D Minor Scale Audio F35

• Warm-up your voice on D minor scale and then sing “All The Pretty Little Horses” song.

• Today, we are going to sing a song written in D minor. Does this song have a brighter and merrier sound or a darker and sadder sound? Can you identify the difference between the “Mama Paquita” song and the “All The Pretty Little Horses song”?

• On this page, point out and circle the dotted quarter notes.

Let's have fun learning piano

The staff has five lines and four spaces. Here is what the staff looks like. It is important to note that the staff is named based on the clef sign that is placed on it. For example - When the treble clef is placed on the staff, the entire staff can be referred to as the "treble staff." The same thing happens when the bass clef is placed on the staff.

The first musical symbol that appears at the beginning of every music staff is a clef symbol. Clefs assign individual notes to certain lines or spaces. It tells us which note (A, B, C, D, E, F, or G) is found on each line or space. "Clef" is the French word for "key."

Bass Clef

The bass clef symbol looks like a backward C with two dots. At the piano, all the bass clef notes must be played with the left hand. The bass clef can also be called the F clef. The bass clef marks the fourth line of the musical staff as F. All other notes fall on the other lines and spaces accordingly.

Where Are Bass Notes

Bass notes normally fall below Middle C. Sometimes the notes may come above middle C, but that is a rare occurrence. Middle C is the cut-off between the two clefs. Look at the image, and you will see that the notes on the bass clef are almost always below Middle C. Middle C is almost always where the bass clef starts.

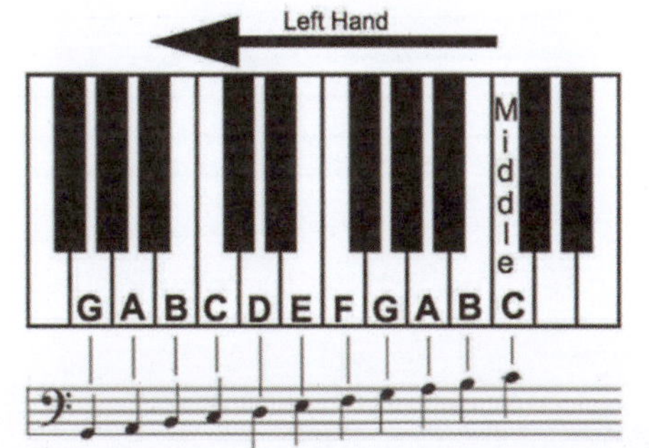

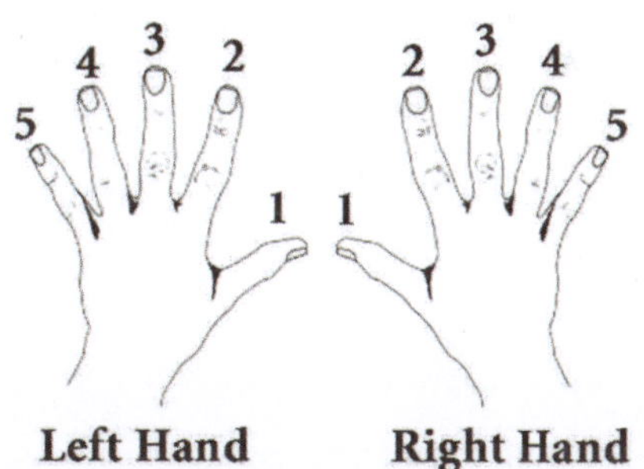

Video L26 Learn to play the "Alphabet Song" on the piano. Please watch Video L26.

The Staff - Bass Clef

The bass clef (also known as F clef) looks like this:

The bass clef gives a landmark on the note F on the 4th line of the bass staff.

Notes are named after the first seven letters of the alphabet (A through G).

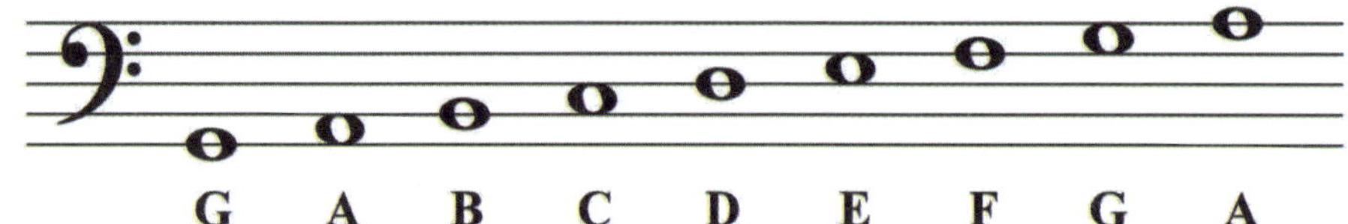

How to draw a bass clef sign

Try drawing the bass clef sign by tracing over the dotted lines, and then draw seven more of your own.

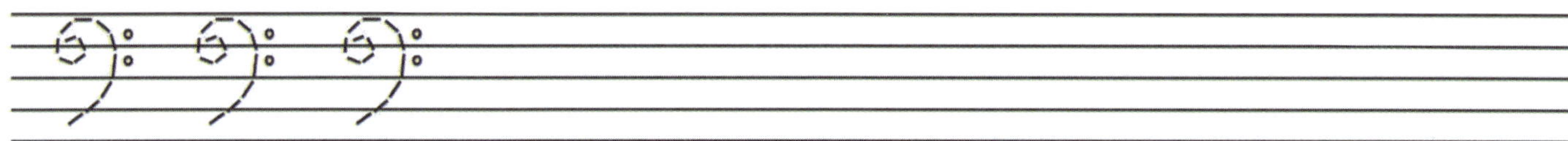

Draw a bass clef at the beginning of the staff, and then write the letter names of each note.

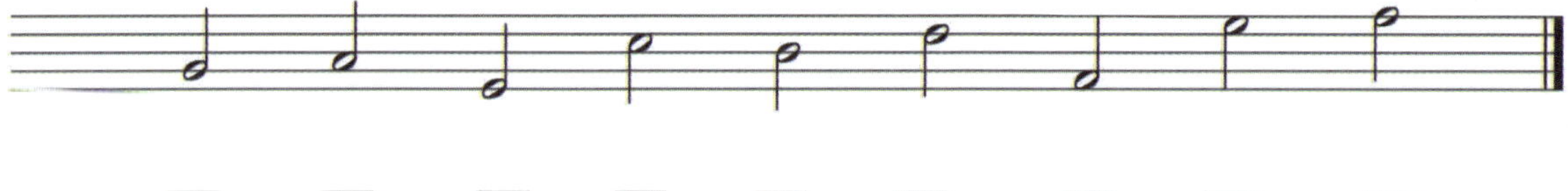

__ __ __ __ __ __ __ __ __

Draw a treble clef at the beginning of the staff, and then draw the indicated notes. If a note can be written at more than one place on the staff, prefer a single spot.

G D E A F B C G A D C

Treble Clef and Bass Clef Note Reading

At the beginning of every staff, you will find a clef sign which gives a letter name to a definite line or space. A clef tells us which note (A, B, C, D, E, F, or G) is found on each line or space.

The treble clef symbol or G clef sign gives the letter name G to the second line of the staff. On any staff, notes are properly arranged so that the next letter is always on the next higher line or space. The last note letter, G, is always followed by another A.

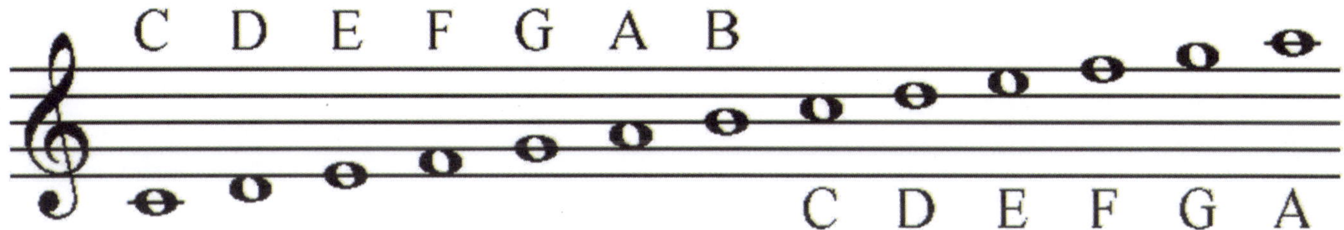

The bass clef can also be called the F clef. The bass clef marks the fourth line of the musical staff as F. All other notes fall on the other lines and spaces accordingly.

Please name the following notes on the indicated space.

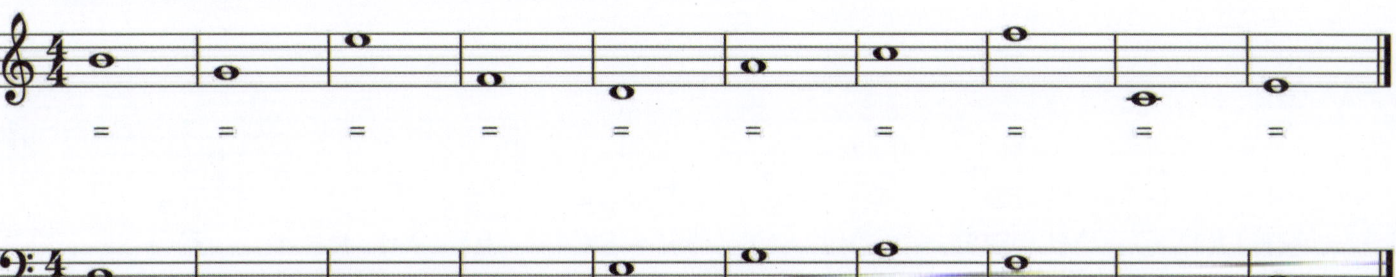

What is A Cappella Music?

A cappella music is a group or solo performance without instrumental accompaniment. In this lesson, we will learn about the history of this singing style and what kind of vocal a cappella music is sung today.

A cappella arrived in English from Italian sometime around the late-18th century. In Italian, a cappella means "in chapel or choir style."

A cappella music at the beginning was heard in churches. Gregorian chants are one example of a cappella style music that was performed in churches. Some churches do not believe that instruments should be used inside of chapels; therefore, they use a cappella arrangements instead of traditional accompaniments.

Enjoy listening *Trois chœurs a capella Opus 42* by Johannes Brahms.

- The following exercise combines pitch and rhythm.
- Chant the rhythm first and then add a pitch. Repeat if necessary.
- Sing pitches, so they are smooth and connected.
- Review the steps for a good singing posture.

- Stand with feet apart
- Knees unlocked
- Back straight
- Rib cage lifted
- Shoulders relaxed
- Hands at your side

Music Key Signatures

In musical notation, a key signature tells you which notes to be played or sung sharpened or flatted throughout the piece and the main tonality or key of the piece.

The keys of C major and A minor have no sharps or flats, therefore no key signature. The key signature is indicated after the treble or bass clef at the beginning of staff or after a double bar line—this separation is necessary to indicate the change in signature—within a staff. In Western tonality, specific groupings represent major and minor keys.

Here's how to find the key signature in a song:

For keys with sharps—the last sharp in the key signature is the leading tone or 7th scale degree of the key. Count up one semitone to get to the tonic.

For keys with flats—the second to last flat is the root of the key.

Let us take a look at G major and E minor key signatures. Notice that the sharp sign is over the F line in the treble clef as well as the bass clef.

G Major (E Minor) Key Signatures

This means that every time the F note appears, it will be raised by a semitone to F sharp.

Another example is the key of F Major and D minor. Notice the flat sign over the B line in both the treble and bass clef? It flattens the B note by a semitone. So, every time the B note appears, the flat B note is played.

F Major (D Minor) Key Signatures

Key signature aids in reducing the accidentals, which are pretty frequent in their absence. They make reading music much easier.

Key Signatures major and relative minor

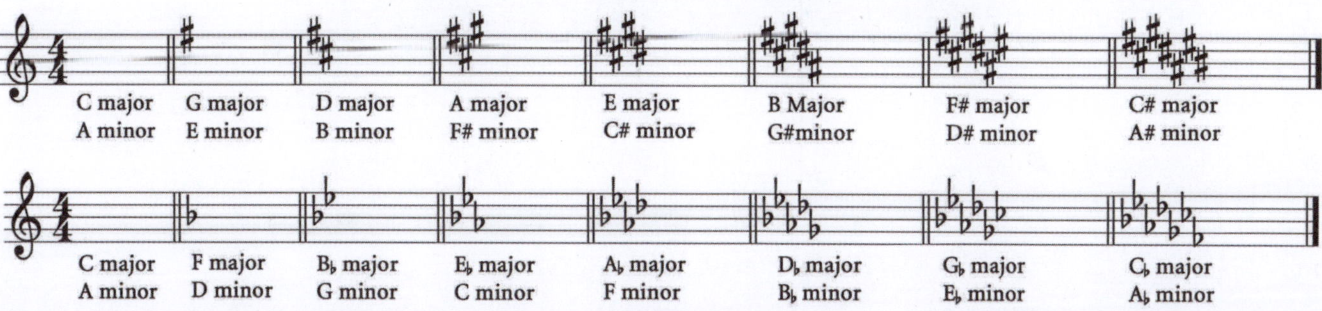

Slurs and Ties

A slur is a curved line that connects two or more notes of different pitches. Slur means the notes should be played as smoothly as possible, without any space in between.

A tie is a curved line that connects two notes of the same pitch; it stands for holding the note for combined rhythmic value of the two notes, as if they were one.

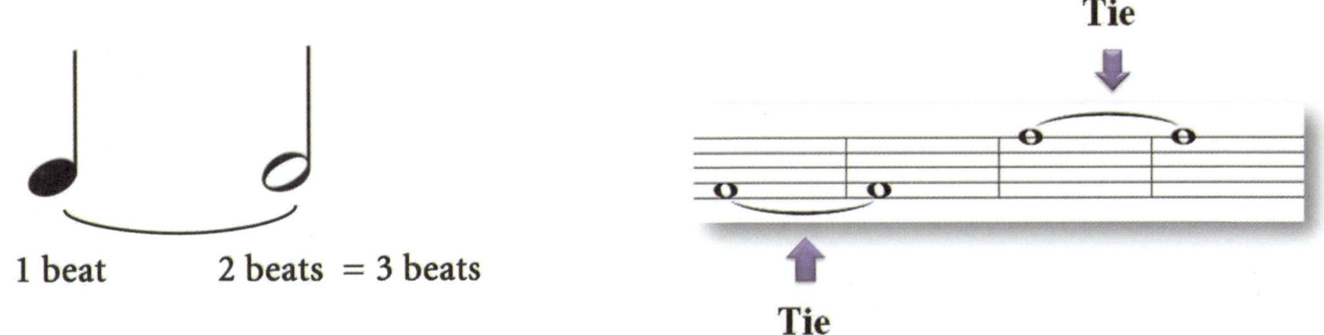

Tied notes are placed on two adjacent notes of the same pitch and are played as one single note.

On each line, write the number of counts each pair of tied notes would receive.

Note	Beats	Note	Beats
𝅝	4 beats	𝅝 .	6 beats
𝅗𝅥	2 beats	𝅗𝅥 .	3 beats
♩	1 beat	♩ .	1½ beats
♪	½ beat	♪ .	¾ beat

𝅗𝅥‿♩ = ______ beats   𝅗𝅥‿♪ = ______ beats

𝅝‿𝅝 = ______ beats   ♪‿♪ = ______ beats

𝅝‿♩ = ______ beats   𝅗𝅥.‿♩ = ______ beats

𝅗𝅥‿𝅗𝅥 = ______ beats   ♪‿♩ = ______ beats

Baroque Music

The baroque era is one of the richest and most diverse periods in music history. Baroque music is a style of Western art music that spanned roughly 1600 to 1750. The baroque era followed the Renaissance music era and was followed by the Classical music era, with the galant style marking the transition between the Baroque and Classical period. The term "Baroque" is derived from the Portuguese word "barroco," which means "misshapen pearl." Johann Sebastian Bach and George Frideric Handel are the notable composers of the Baroque era. Domenico Scarlatti, Antonio Vivaldi, Claudio Monteverdi, Heinrich Schütz, and Johann Pachelbel, along with some other composers, are notable mentions of this era. Baroque music expanded the size, range, and complexity of instrumental performance and established opera, cantata, oratorio, concerto, and sonata as musical genres.

Baroque music is noted for its distinct variations in dynamics, loud and quiet, blending solos and ensembles, and varying complexity and texture sounds. The Baroque period was a period of innovation and expansion of music. Composers used many different forms and complicated variations. Composers were often indicating the instruments on which a piece should be played instead of allowing the performer to choose. Most pieces follow a fast-slow-fast format and are notoriously difficult to play. Interesting instruments like the trumpet and violin also grew in popularity.

The Baroque Music Library

Harpsichord

Baroque theatre in Č
Ceský Krumlov

Heinrich Schütz

Heinrich Schütz was a German composer and organist who is widely regarded as the most important German composer before J.S. Bach. Along with Claudio Monteverdi, is widely regarded as one of the most important composers of the 17th century. He wrote what is believed to be the first German opera, Dafne, which was performed in Torgau in 1627, but the music has since been lost.

Moritz von Hessen-Kassel discovered Heinrich Schütz's musical abilities in 1599.

He studied law in Marburg before moving to Venice in 1609 to study music with Giovanni Gabrieli. He stayed in Venice until 1613 with Giovanni Gabrieli. His most well-known works are in sacred music, ranging from solo voice with instrumental accompaniment to A Cappella choral music. Representative works include his three books of *Symphoniae Sacrae*, the *Psalms of David*, the *Sieben Worte Jesu Christi am Kreuz* (the Seven Last Words on the Cross) and his three *Passion* settings.

Coloring Time...Fun...Fun

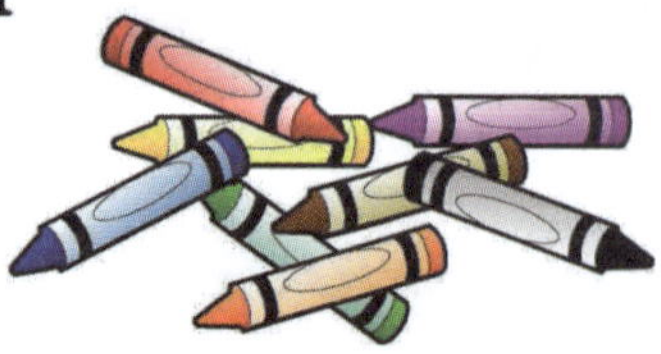

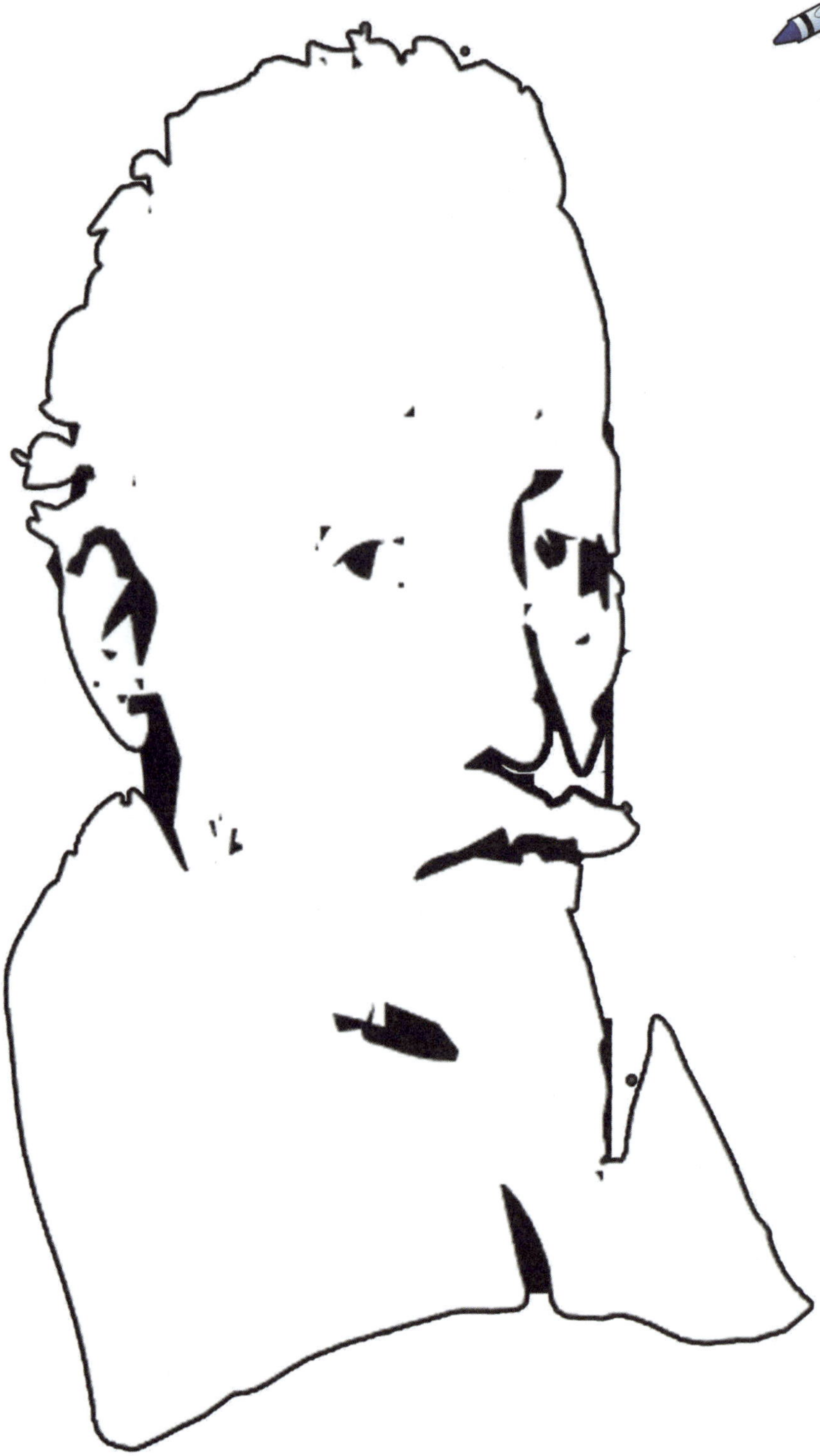

Heinrich Schütz

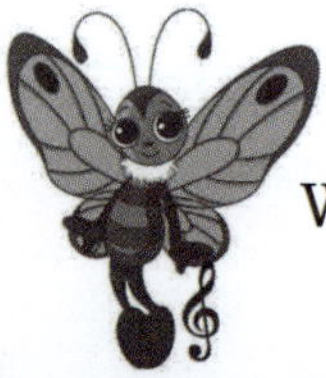

While coloring, you may listen to *Psalms of David,* composed by Heinrich Schütz.

Heinrich Schütz Quiz

1. Heinrich Schütz was a ____________ composer and organist.
   a) Russian
   b) French
   c) German

2. Heinrich Schütz is often considered to be one of the most important composers of the 17th century alongside ____________________________.
   a) Claude Debussy
   b) Claudio Monteverdi
   c) Sergei Rachmaninoff

3. Heinrich Schütz's musical talents were discovered by Moritz von Hessen-Kassel in 1599.
   a) True
   b) Flase

4. Heinrich Schütz composed ____________________________.
   a) *Fur Elise*
   b) *Moonlight Sonata*
   c) *Psalms of David*

The Staff - High and Low

Music is written on a staff of five lines and the four spaces between these lines. The lines on the staff are numbered from bottom to top. The spaces between lines are numbered from bottom to top.

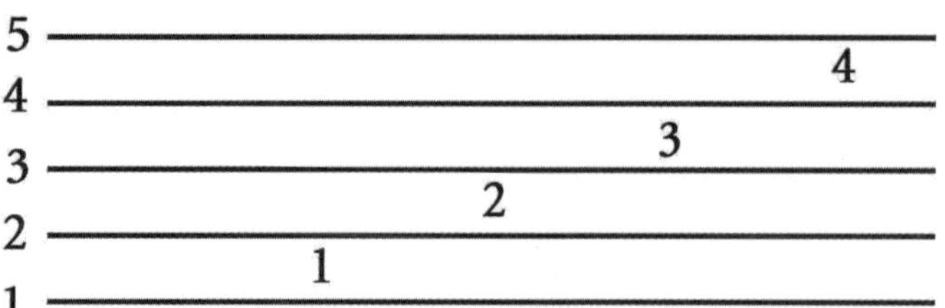

Musical sounds (low or high) are represented by the position of notes on the staff. Notes which are higher on the staff have a higher sound or pitch, compared to those lower on the staff.

The first note sounds lower than the second note.

The first note sounds higher than the second note.

Draw a note on the indicated line or space, then circle the highest note you drew on the staff.

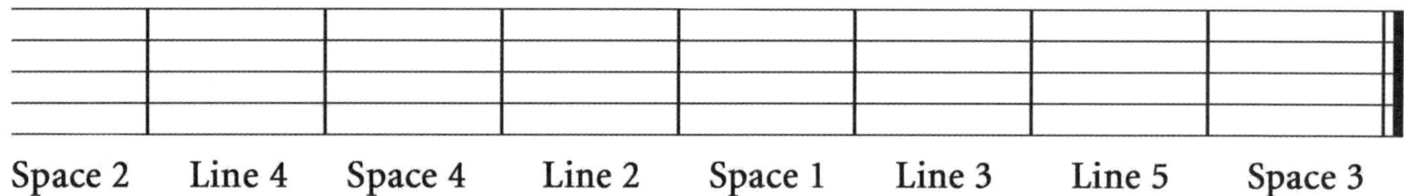

Use an arrow to indicate whether the second note of each measure sounds higher ↗ or lower ↘ in pitch than the first note. You can also listen to Audio F39 **Audio F39**

Tone Color

Tone color is the characteristic of sound, which allows us to distinguish one instrument's sound from another. Every instrument produces its own tone color. When you hear a trumpet and a piano play the same pitch, for example, the tone color of each instrument helps you to distinguish between the sounds. Tone color is also sometimes known as timber.

Tone color is the individual sound quality of a voice or instrument. The word "timbre" is used interchangeably with tone color. Both terms mean the same thing.

Types of tone color in music

Here is a brief list of a few different types of tone colors often found in music:

- Vocal music
- A Capella
- Instrumental music
- Acoustic music
- Amplified music – making sound louder through electric amplification
- Electronic music – sounds produced or altered by electronic devices

String Family of the Orchestra

The strings are the largest family of instruments in the orchestra and they come in four sizes: the violin, which is the smallest, followed by viola and cello, and the largest of them all, the double bass, sometimes also called the contrabass.

Violin is one of the primary instruments in classical music and orchestras. In an orchestra there are more violins than any other instrument. Orchestras have two sections of violins known as the first and second violins, each section playing a different part. In a modern orchestra, there are usually 16 violinists in the violins I section and 14 in the violins II section. A conventionalized violin is 24 inches (two feet) long, with a slightly longer bow. You play the violin by resting it between your chin and left shoulder. Your left-hand holds the neck of the violin and presses down the strings to change the pitch while your right-hand moves the bow or plucks the strings.

Audio F40

You may listen Piotr Ilich Tchaikovsky - *Violin Concerto in D major, Op. 35*

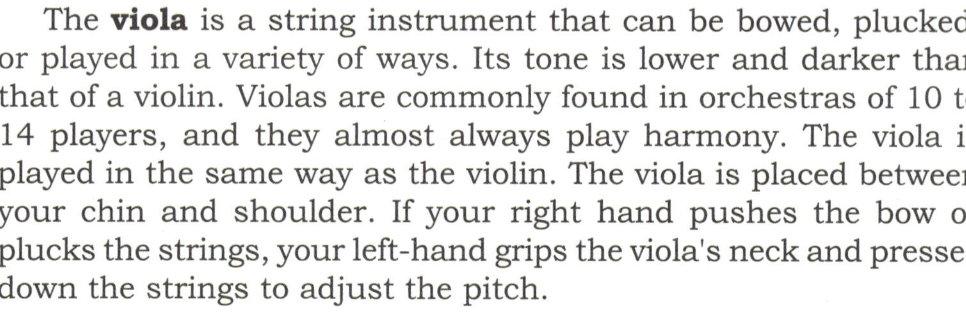

The **viola** is a string instrument that can be bowed, plucked, or played in a variety of ways. Its tone is lower and darker than that of a violin. Violas are commonly found in orchestras of 10 to 14 players, and they almost always play harmony. The viola is played in the same way as the violin. The viola is placed between your chin and shoulder. If your right hand pushes the bow or plucks the strings, your left-hand grips the viola's neck and presses down the strings to adjust the pitch.

You may listen to *Viola Concerto in G,* by Georg Philipp Telemann

 Audio F41

Cello looks like violin and viola but is much larger in size (around 4 feet long) and has thicker strings than both violin and viola. Cello sound can create a melancholy mood. In an orchestra, there are 8 to 12 cellos. You play cello sitting down on a chair, keeping the body of the cello between your knees and the neck is resting on the left shoulder. The body of the cello rests on the ground and is supported by a metal peg. The cello has four strings, C, G, D, A. Most cello music is written in the bass clef and sometimes moves into tenor clef as the music gets higher. Sometimes if the melody is very high, the treble clef is used.

You may listen to *Cello Concerto in B minor Op.104,* composed by Antonin Dvorak

 Audio F42

Double Bass is more than six feet high, and is the largest member of the string family, with the longest strings that allow it to play extremely low notes. In an orchestra, there are 6 to 8 double basses. To play the double bass, you must stand up or sit on a very tall stool. Similar to cello, the body of the double bass rests on the floor, supported by a metal peg. The neck of the double bass rests on your left shoulder. The sound is produced just like on a cello, using the left hand to change pitch and the right to move the bow or pluck the string.

You may listen to *Concerto for Double Bass No 2 in B Minor,* composed by Giovanni Bottesini.

 Audio F43

Clap the rhythm

Audio F44

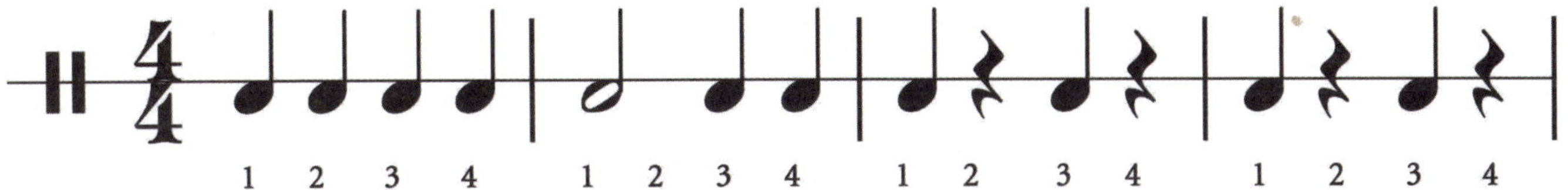

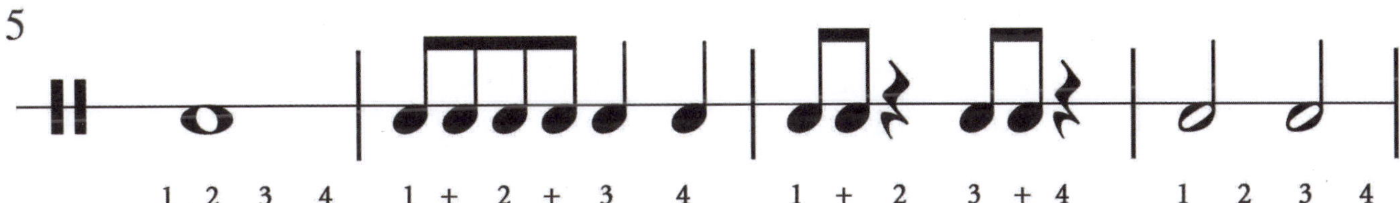

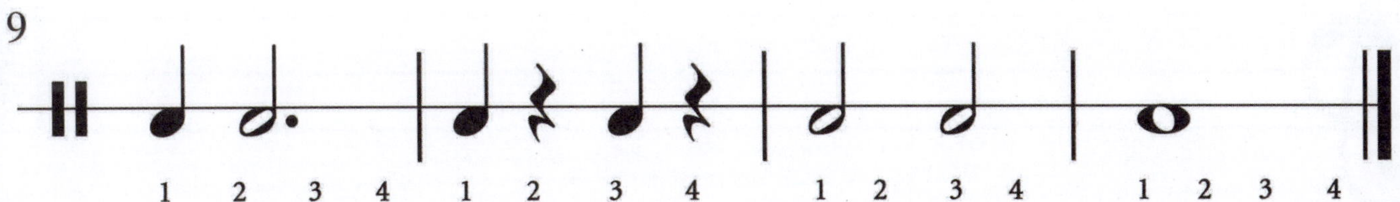

- Practice clapping the rhythm with a metronome.
- Children discover what is meant by a steady beat.
- They experience the beat through physical movement as they move their bodies in line with the music.
- Clap the rhythm at a variety of different speeds.
- Try to make your rhythm; please give at least one example.

Treble Clef

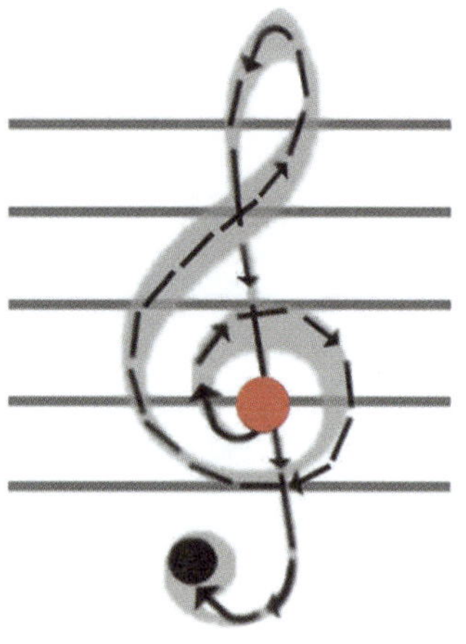

How to draw a treble clef

Start on the G line (2nd line up) where the red dot is and follow the arrow around, up and back down.

Let us draw a treble clef.

Bass Clef

How to draw the Bass Clef

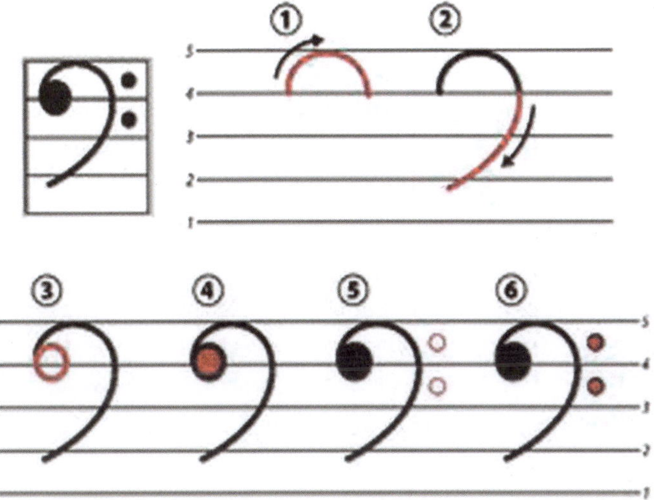

Let us draw a Bass Clef.

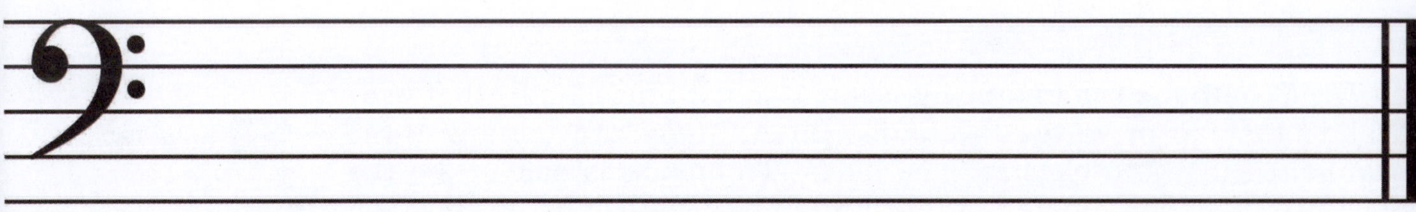

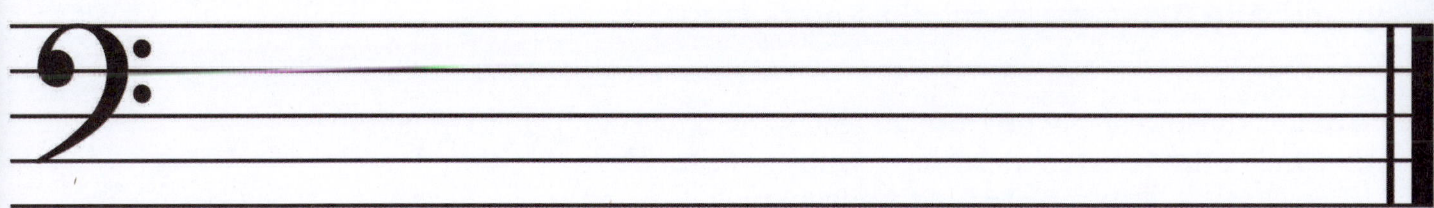

Brass Family

A major family of instruments is the brass instrument family. A brass family includes trumpets, trombones, French horns, euphoniums, and tubas. The brass family of instruments is made with brass, which is a type of metal that is generally muted gold in color.

These brass instruments have a set of valves that the player presses. When they do this, their air travels through new parts of tubing, which changes the sound/pitch of the instrument. The longer the air has to travel, the lower the sound. The shorter- the higher! The sound starts on a brass family instrument when a musician buzzes their lips into the mouthpiece to get the air inside vibrating.

The **trumpet** is considered the oldest brass instrument in existence, has been around since 1500 BC. Throughout history, the trumpet has been used to gather people together as a call to war, to sound alarms, and to add luster to any parade. The trumpet, like the violin, is the smallest member of its family and, with its vivid and lively tone, plays the highest pitches. The trumpet is a slender brass pipe with three attached valves; all are curved and bent into long loops. If you stretch out the trumpet to its full length, it would be 6 ½ feet long! In Orchestra, there are 2 to 4 trumpets. The trumpet is played by blowing into the mouthpiece and making a "buzzing" sound.

Audio F45

French Horn is a brass instrument that is somewhat larger than a trumpet hence has a lower pitch. Interestingly, the French horn is a German instrument! The instrument dates back to the early 1600s. The design was much more straightforward at that time. It was just a circular horn made from a single tube with a mouthpiece and flared bell. The French horn is a brass instrument made from metal. The French horn's 20 feet of tubing is rolled up into a circular shape, with a large bell at its end.

Audio F46

The **Trombone** is a unique instrument in the brass family that uses a slide instead of valves to change pitch. There are usually three trombones in the orchestra. The oldest Trombone is said to be the Sackbutt, which originated in Belgium around the 1450s. In the 19th century, Trombones were introduced into early Jazz music. In the 21st century, Trombone can be classified into five ranges. They are the Soprano, Alto, Tenor, Bass, and the Contrabass.

Audio F47

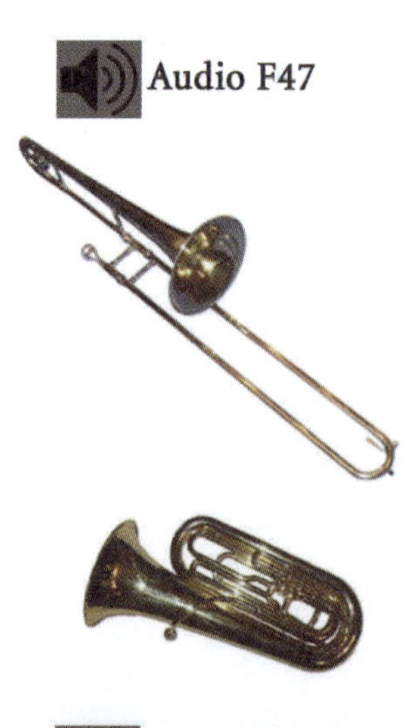

Tuba is the lowest-pitched and largest of the brass family instruments and is one of the latest modern-day symphony orchestra addition. Built of brass that is electroplated with silver, nickel, or copper, there are many variations in Tuba like the contrabass tubas, bass tubas, tenor tuba, and sub contrabass tubas. Made of about 16 feet of tubing, the Tuba has three to five valves and is held upright in the player's lap.

Audio F48

Different Voice Types and How to Distinguish Between Them

Have you ever wonder what the difference is between a soprano and a mezzo-soprano, or which voice type can sing the lowest notes? Most opera singers fall into the voice category, which identifies the singer's ability as well as the requirements of a specific role.

How do we categorize a soprano, mezzo-soprano, tenor, or bass, the four most common types of voices? It all depends upon one's vocal range or the difference from the lowest to the highest note that a particular singer can produce. Singer's range variation is directly related to the size of vocal cords and the speed at which they vibrate. Other factors determining the signer's voice are the consistency of timbre (sound quality or color of the voice) and the ability to project voice over a full orchestra — remember, there are no microphones in opera, and there are small, medium/large, and extra-large voices.

Soprano

For females, the soprano is the highest voice type. In operatic drama, the soprano is almost always the heroine because she projects innocence and youth. In this category, there are other sub-divisions, such as coloratura soprano, lyric soprano, and dramatic soprano.

Mezzo-soprano Audio F50

Mezzo-sopranos have a darker, heavier tone than sopranos. The mezzo-soprano is the middle female voice and the most common of the female singing voices. There are three types of mezzo-soprano, coloratura mezzo, dramatic mezzo, and lyric mezzo. One of the most well-known roles for a dramatic mezzo is the fiery gypsy "Carmen" in the opera of the same name.

Tenor Audio F51

In an opera, the tenor is the highest male voice and is often the hero or the love interest of the plot. There are several different types of tenor voices, lyric and dramatic tenors. Lyric tenors have a high voice, bright tones, and dramatic tenors have a darker sound with a ringing quality in the upper range and are regarded as the most common ones. Famous tenors include Enrico Caruso, Juan Diego Flórez, Alfredo Kraus, and Luciano Pavarotti.

Baritone Audio F52

Thc baritone is the most popular male voice, with a range that falls somewhere between high tenor and low bass. This voice has a dramatic quality to it, with the ability to produce deep, dark tones. Favorite roles for baritones include the hunchback court jester in *Rigoletto* (dramatic) and the famous Toréador Escamillo in *Carmen.*

Let's compose a short melody

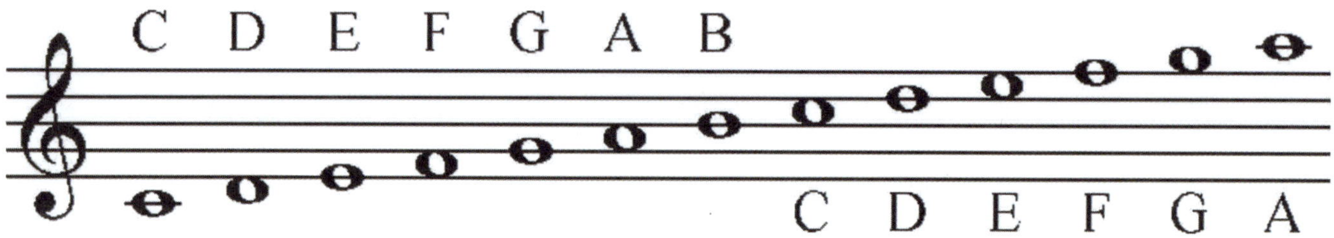

C D E F G A B

C D E F G A

2

4

6

- Write six measures, melody, and rhythm using the given opening example.
- Every measure has to have four beats.
- Have fun composing the song.
- Sing each musical note by respecting the notes' values of your composition.

Music Ensemble

A musical ensemble, also known as a musical group, is a group of people who perform instrumental or vocal music. There are different kinds of ensembles that are identified upon their played music, the number of musicians performing together, and instruments they use in their performances. Small ensembles are groups of musicians that may vary from two to eight in number: the specific compositions associated with small ensembles dictate musical instruments' set to be used. Types of musical ensembles can be a marching band, an orchestra, a jazz ensemble, a rock band, an a cappella group, etc."

Audio F53

Duet

A composition for two performers is called a duet. The performers contribute equally to the piece. They take turns performing a solo section rather than simultaneous performance. In classical music, the term is often used for a composition for two singers or pianists performing together. A piece performed by two pianists together on the same piano is referred to as "piano duet" or "piano four hands."

Audio F54

Trio

Trios are three musicians performing together specific pieces of music meant to be played by three musicians or pieces of music meant for three instruments. For example, a string trio is composed of a cello, violin, and viola. You may listen to a trio example.

Audio F55

Quartet

Quartets are four musicians performing together, or compositions meant to be played by four musicians, or a piece for four instruments. For example, a string quartet is an ensemble of four solo strings, traditionally two violins, viola, and cello.

Audio F56

Choral Groups

A group of singers performing together as a group is called a choir or chorus. The former term is often used for groups affiliated with a church (whether or not they actually occupy the choir), and the second refers to groups that perform in theaters or concert halls. Choirs can sing both with and without instrumental accompaniment. Singing without accompaniment is called A Cappella singing.

Let's practice writing musical notes

Practice writing musical notes. Each measure has one musical note written at the beginning; continue writing the same musical note.

Tempo

How does the speed of a song affect our emotions? How can we determine the speed of a song simply by looking at it? We can find this out by learning about the tempo! The tempo is defined as the pace or speed at which a section of music is played.

Tempos, or tempi, help the composer convey a feeling of either intensity or relaxation. Composers first started to indicate precise tempo recommendations in the 19th century. The German inventor and clocksmith Diederich Nicolaus Winkel (1777-1826) is known to have built the first metronome in 1814. He showed it to his friend J.N. Mälzel, who patented it the following year.

A tempo marking indicates the actual duration of the time values. One rhythm structure can be written in various ways, for example:

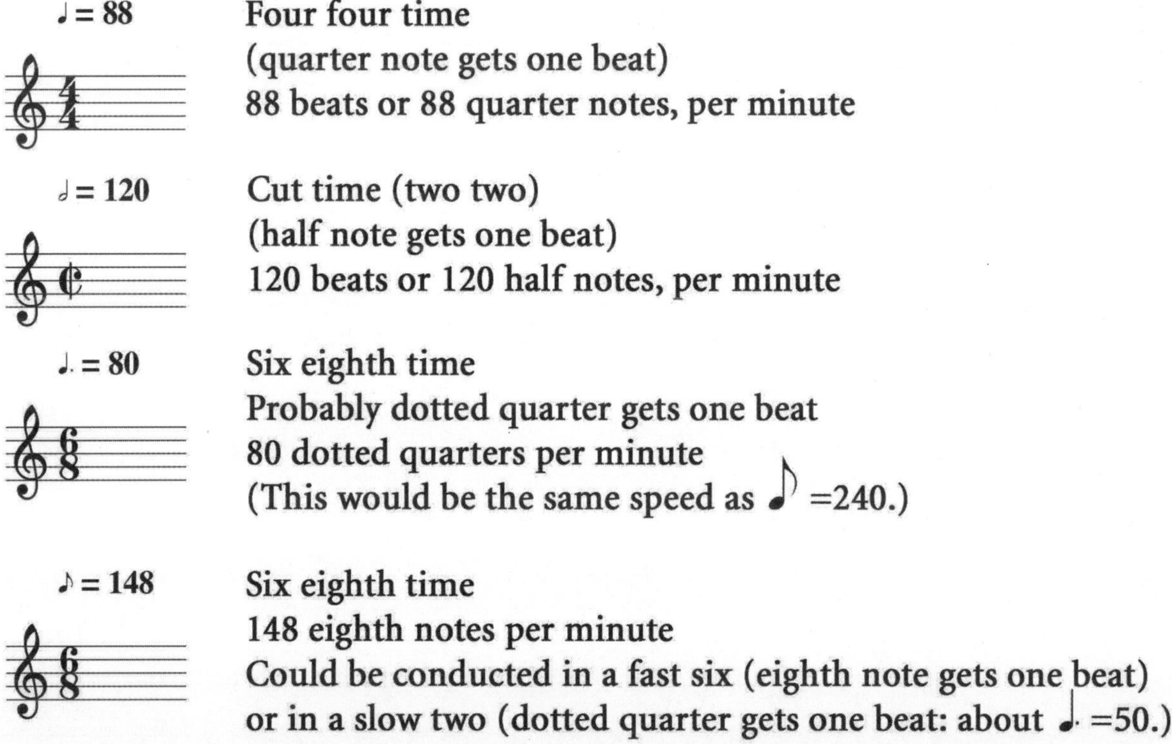

The numbers indicate the number of beats per minute, often abbreviated as MM (as in "Metronom Mälzel") or the somewhat vague BPM (as in beats per minute or bars per minute). The metronome marking is written at the beginning of the work above the time signature and usually has the same note value as the bottom number of the time signature.

Practice singing this exercise at different speed tempos.

Audio F57

Glossary of Tempo Markings used in Classical Music

In classical music the most common tempo markings are in Italian, though sometimes French and German are also used.

Tempo Markings - Italian	Definition	Beats per minute (bpm)
Grave	very slow and solemn	25–45 bpm
Largo	broad, very slow and dignified	40–60 bpm
Adagio	slow, but not as slow as largo	66-76 bpm
Andante	at a walking pace	76–108 bpm
Moderato	moderately	108–120 bpm
Allegretto	moderately fast	112–120 bpm
Allegro moderato	close to but not quite allegro	116–120 bpm
Allegro	fast, quickly, and bright	120–168 bpm
Vivace	lively and fast	168–176 bpm
Presto	very, very fast	168–200 bpm

Terms for tempo change:

Rallentando – gradually slowing down
Ritardando – gradually slowing down (but not as much as rallentando)
Ritenuto – immediately slowing down
Stringendo – gradually speeding up (slowly)
Accelerando – gradually speeding up (quickly)

Audio F58

Coffee Grows on White Oak Trees

♩ = 67

Traditional Song

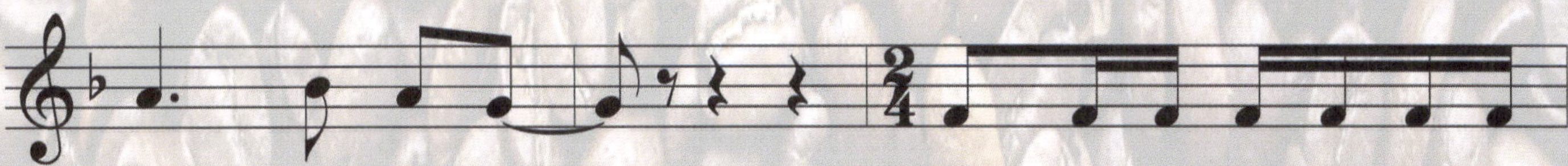

- Practice singing "Coffee Grows on White Oak Trees," with beautiful intonation and expression.
- Practice clapping the rhythm with a metronome.
- Sing with pitch and tuning accuracy.
- Practice singing with a metronome. After you sing "Coffee Grows on White Oak Trees" a few times with the metronome set up at ♩ = 67, you may also try another speed tempo. For instance, ♩ = 80 could be a good option.
- Do you notice the difference in tempo?

Movement Activity

Remove any barriers and make the area child-friendly to create a dance floor. Place all of the props to the side of the room on a table (such as hats, balloons, ribbons, pom-poms, wigs, teddy bears, and flowers). The kids will have to rush to the table and choose a prop as soon as the music starts playing. As long as it is safe, they can also be asked to select some other accessories from the dance room. Then they can dance as they like with the prop as an accessory. They return the prop to the table until the music stops. When the music starts up again, they pick another prop and continue dancing in that style.

It Rained a Mist

Adagio

Traditional Song

D G A7

It rained a mist, It rained a mist, It rained all o - ver the

D G A7 D

town, town, town, It rained ___ all o - ver the town,

Recorder Fingering Chart

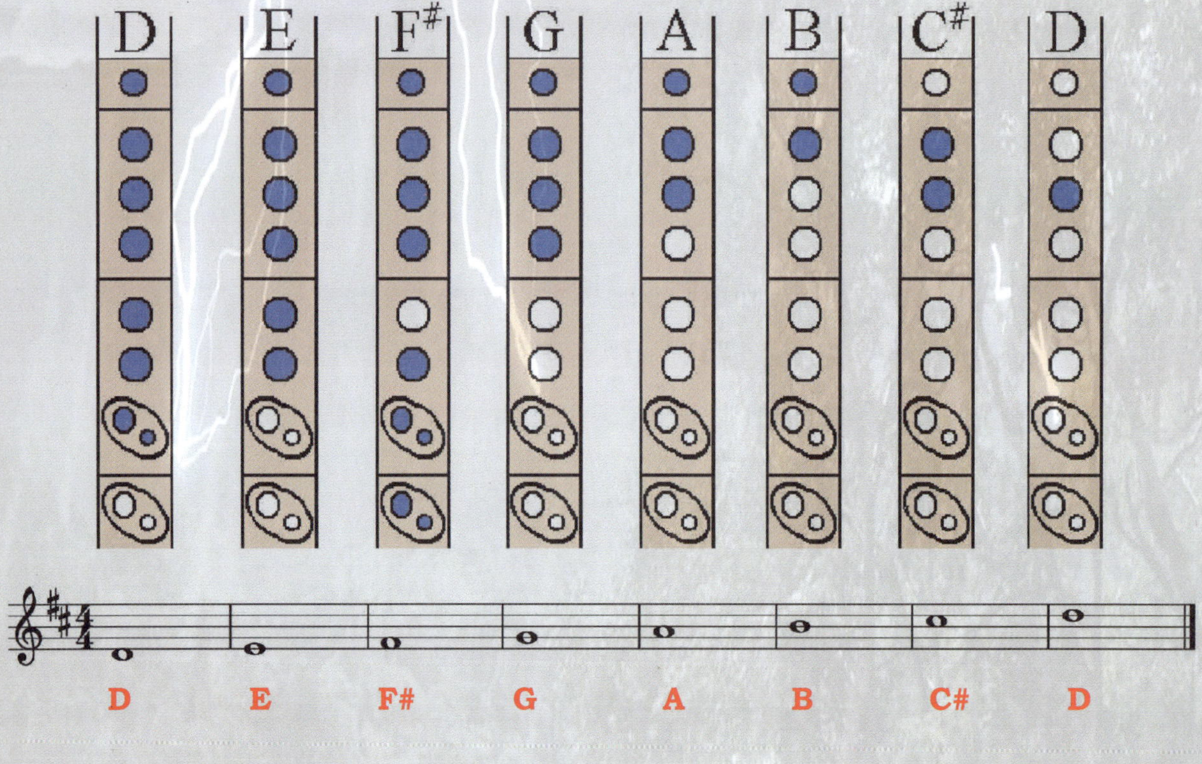

D E F# G A B C# D

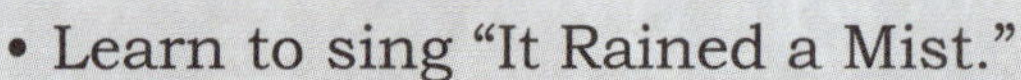

D E F# G A B C# D

• Learn to sing "It Rained a Mist."

• Develop the habit of tapping, patting, or using your chosen moving methods to the basic pulse.

• The important thing is to feel the pulse of the tempo in your head as you sing. Tap your foot if it helps. While listening to music, tap your foot, drum, or clap on your legs, to reinforce that particular instinct for rhythm.

• Manage your breath to establish musically expressive phrasing.

• Sing with a supported tone and avoid breathing at every bar line.

• Practice singing with a metronome at the following tempo: Adagio, Moderato, and Fast.

• Write in the beat below each musical note, and the rest indicated. Then clap the rhythm while counting the beats out loud.

Optional to teach! You can teach students to play "It Rained a Mist" using a musical instrument in the classroom, such as a recorder.

Practice the rhythm and pitch exercise with a metronome.
Notice the changes in tempo?

Tempo Markings

Match the terms to their definitions.

Grave	**at a walking pace**
Moderato	**moderately fast**
Andante	**fast, quickly, and bright**
Allegretto	**very slow and solemn**
Presto	**lively and fast**
Allegro	**moderately**
Vivace	**slow, but not as slow as largo**
Adagio	**very, very fast**

Luigi Boccherini

Luigi Boccherini (born in Lucca, 19 February 1743; died in Madrid, 28 May 1805) was a famous Italian cellist and composer of the Classical era. Luigi Boccherini's father, a professional bass player, was his first teacher. He also studied from the Abbé Vannucci, chapel master, to the Archbishop. Boccherini proved to be a talented pupil. In 1757 he moved to Rome to perfect his technique under more expert teachers.

He returned to Lucca as a virtuoso cellist after completing his studies in Rome and joining the town theatre orchestra. At the same time, he demonstrated his skill as a composer by performing a special concert devoted entirely to Boccherini's sonatas, which he organized with the help of violinist Filippo Manfredi. The concert was a huge success, so he and Manfredi decided to tour all the big French cities. They were successful everywhere, including Paris, where they conducted a concert in 1768.

Before moving to Paris and then Spain, Boccherini worked in Vienna. He was named court composer to King Friedrich Wilhelm II of Prussia, who was himself an expert cellist and was in the service of the Infante Don Luis and numerous other patrons.

Boccherini was strongly influenced by Haydn's style. During his long career, Boccherini wrote an impressive number of large-scale chamber works. His compositions include 91 string quartets (Haydn wrote 83), an astonishing 137 quintets for various combinations of strings, multitudes of trios, keyboard quintets, sextets, sonatas, and other works. As a virtuoso cellist, Boccherini wrote a dozen exceptional concertos for cello that are very little known today. Boccherini's 30 symphonies, like everyone else's from this period, pale in comparison to Haydn's and Mozart's, but they are still fun, welcoming, and sometimes surprising imaginative.

Coloring Time...Fun...Fun

Luigi Boccherini

Audio F62

While coloring, you may listen to *Minuetto,* composed by Luigi Boccherini.

Luigi Boccherini Quiz

1. Which country was Luigi Boccherini born in?
a) Germany
b) Italy
c) France

2. Luigi Boccherini was a ____________________ composer.
a) Baroque
b) Romantic
c) Classical
d) Renaissance

3. Luigi Boccherini was famous and influential as a virtuoso ____________________.
a) Pianist
b) Cellist
c) Opera singer

4. Boccherini admired Haydn greatly and was strongly influenced by Haydn's style.
a) True
b) False

Music of Malaysia

"Music of Malaysia" is the generic term for various Malaysian genres. A wide variety of genres in Malaysian music reflect the specific ethnic groups of multiracial Malaysian society consisting of Malay, Indian, Iban, Chinese, Dayak, Kadazandusun, Eurasians, and other groups.

Malaysia stands out as a country with people from many different cultures and nationalities. Despite its sheer diverse culture, Malaysia has managed to carve an identity for itself in the world. Although the national language of the country is Malay, it is English, which is widely spoken and understood by the people in the country. Though the predominant religion is Islam in Malaysia, there are people belonging to all different religions here. All festivals are celebrated with equal joy and fervor in this enchantingly rich land. Architecture and music are two pillars of Malaysian culture.

Petronas Twin Towers

POD Pavilion Kuala Lumpur

Malaysia International Trade and Exhibition Centre

In old times, music was used as a form of communication during special occasions. There used to be different drumbeats to announce a birth, death, wedding, or any danger in the villages. As a multi-cultural country, different people have been inclined towards different compositions like Indian, Chinese, Portuguese, and others.

Gradually, with the passage of time, Malaysian music managed to etch an identity for itself. Zapin music inspired by Arabia is loved by people throughout the country. Nowadays, the present generation is developing a taste for European and American music, and as a result, many pop singers, along with several rock bands, have sprung up. Looking over at the Malaysian traditional music, which comes from Gamelan that is an ensemble of gongs, drums, and xylophones alongside rebab, which is a stringed instrument that produces an ethereal and soft sound, it is concluded that Malaysian music is diverse. Today, Rebana Ubi is the ceremonial instrument that is played quite often for striking, refined music.

Audio F63 Malay Traditional Song - Zapin Ghalit

Musical Notes

Treble Clef Line Notes

Treble Clef Space Notes

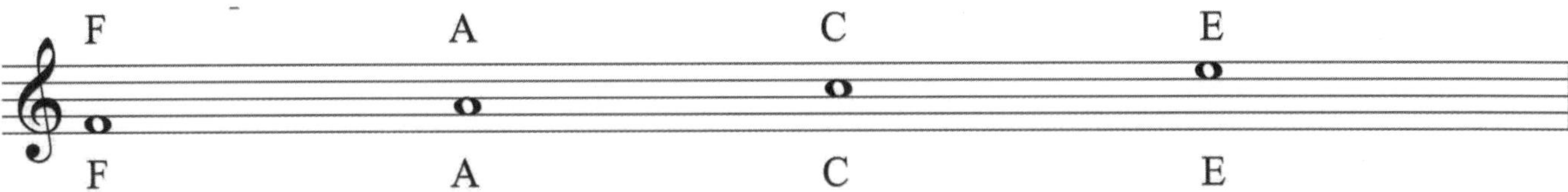

Bass Clef Line Notes

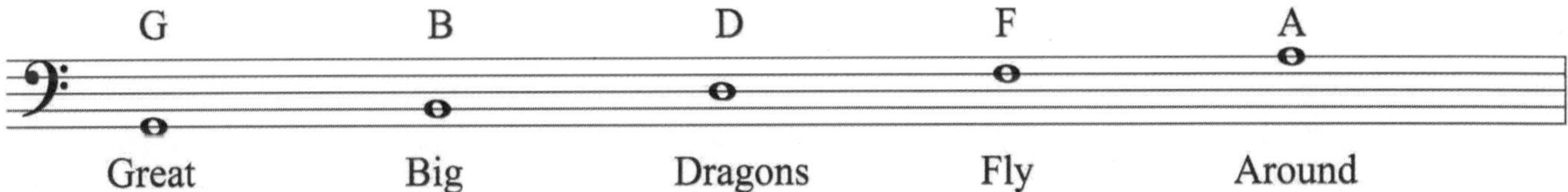

Bass Clef Space Notes

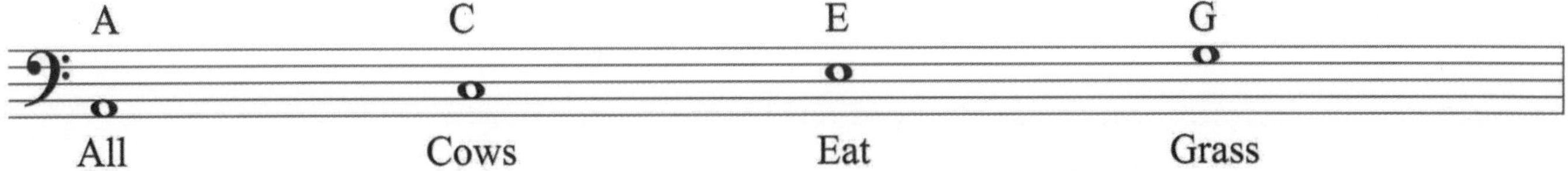

Please write the name of each musical note on the indicated space.

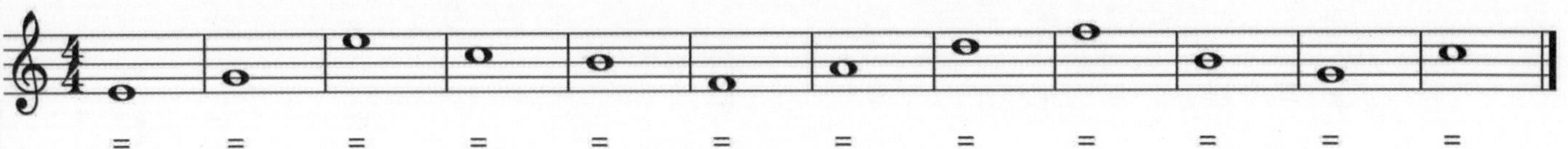

= = = = = = = = = = = =

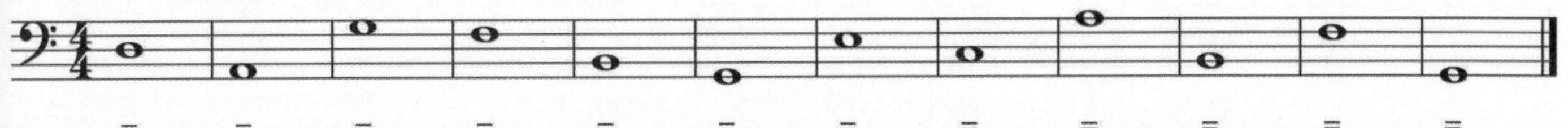

= = = = = = = = = = = =

Musical Dynamics

Dynamics are musical instructions that tell us how loud we can play a musical note. Dynamics are an integral part of conveying a composition's mood. Sometimes a piece will have a few dynamics, and others will have many changes.

Traditionally, dynamic markings are based on Italian words, although there is nothing wrong with simply writing things like "softly" or "louder" in music, still forte (f) stands for loud, and piano (p) means soft.

Dynamic Markings

Term	Symbol:	Effect:
pianissimo	*pp*	very soft
piano	*p*	soft
mezzo piano	*mp*	moderately soft
mezzo forte	*mf*	slightly loud
forte	*f*	loud
fortissimo	*ff*	very loud
fortepiano	*fp*	loud then soft
sforzando	*sfz*	sudden accent
crescendo	<	gradually louder
diminuendo	>	gradually softer

Dynamic Changes

A composer may change the dynamic of a song at any time by simply placing a dynamic name (forte) or abbreviation (f) in the score. Composers often want to gradually decrease or increase the dynamic (volume) of the music to add more intensity to the song.

They will use a crescendo or diminuendo marking symbol. When a composer wants to indicate a dramatic or sudden change in dynamics, he/she may use the term subito (literally "suddenly") as in subito piano or subito fortissimo.

Changes in dynamics can also be modified through additional adjectives:

- diminuendo poco a poco - becoming softer slowly and gradually
- molto crescendo - becoming louder quickly
- decrescendo al niente - becoming soft to the point of silence, fading to nothing

Dynamics and Articulation

Dynamics are used to show how loudly a piece of music must be played. Articulation is used to show how a note should be played or sung - e.g., staccato or slur. Look at the music below for Frédéric Chopin's *Nocturne in C-sharp Minor*. You may also listen to *Nocturne in C-sharp Minor* and try recognizing the dynamics.

What dynamics and articulations do you see?

If there were no dynamics and articulation, then the music would sound completely different. Dynamics and articulations bring the notes to life on a page.

Articulation

Articulation in music refers to how specific notes or passages are played or sung.

Legato means that the notes are smooth and connected when you sing or play them. Notes are joined by curved lines.

Staccato is Italian for "detached." It means that notes should be sung or played short and detached. It is indicated by short vertical strokes or dots above or below the note.

Slur is a symbol in Western musical notation, indicating that the notes it embraces are to be sung or played without separation.

Audio F67

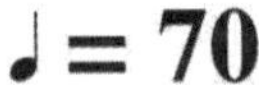

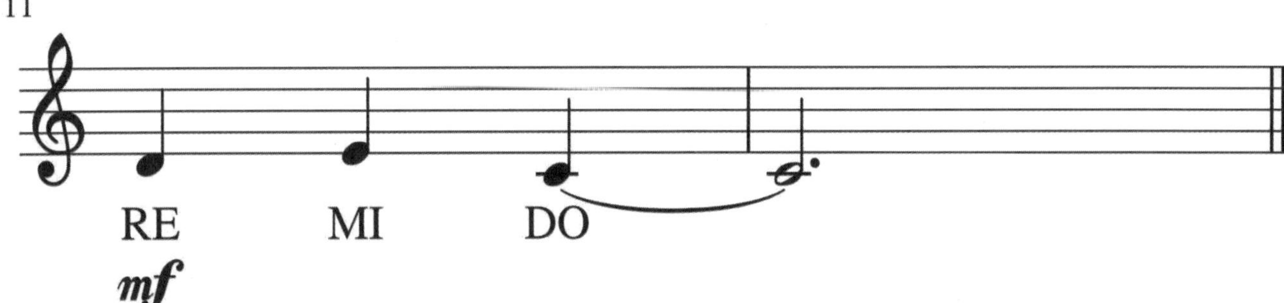

• Practice singing this solfege exercise with beautiful intonation and expression.

• Practice singing with a metronome.

• Pay close attention to the details of pitch and dynamics.

• Point out all dynamic and articulation signs on the music sheet and explain their meaning.

Down In The Valley

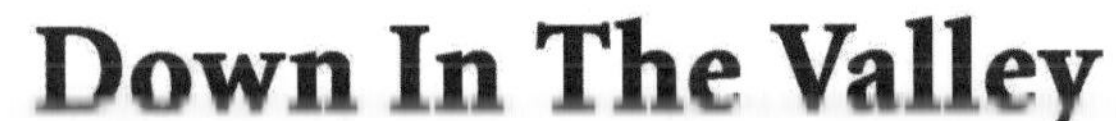

Audio F69

Traditional Song

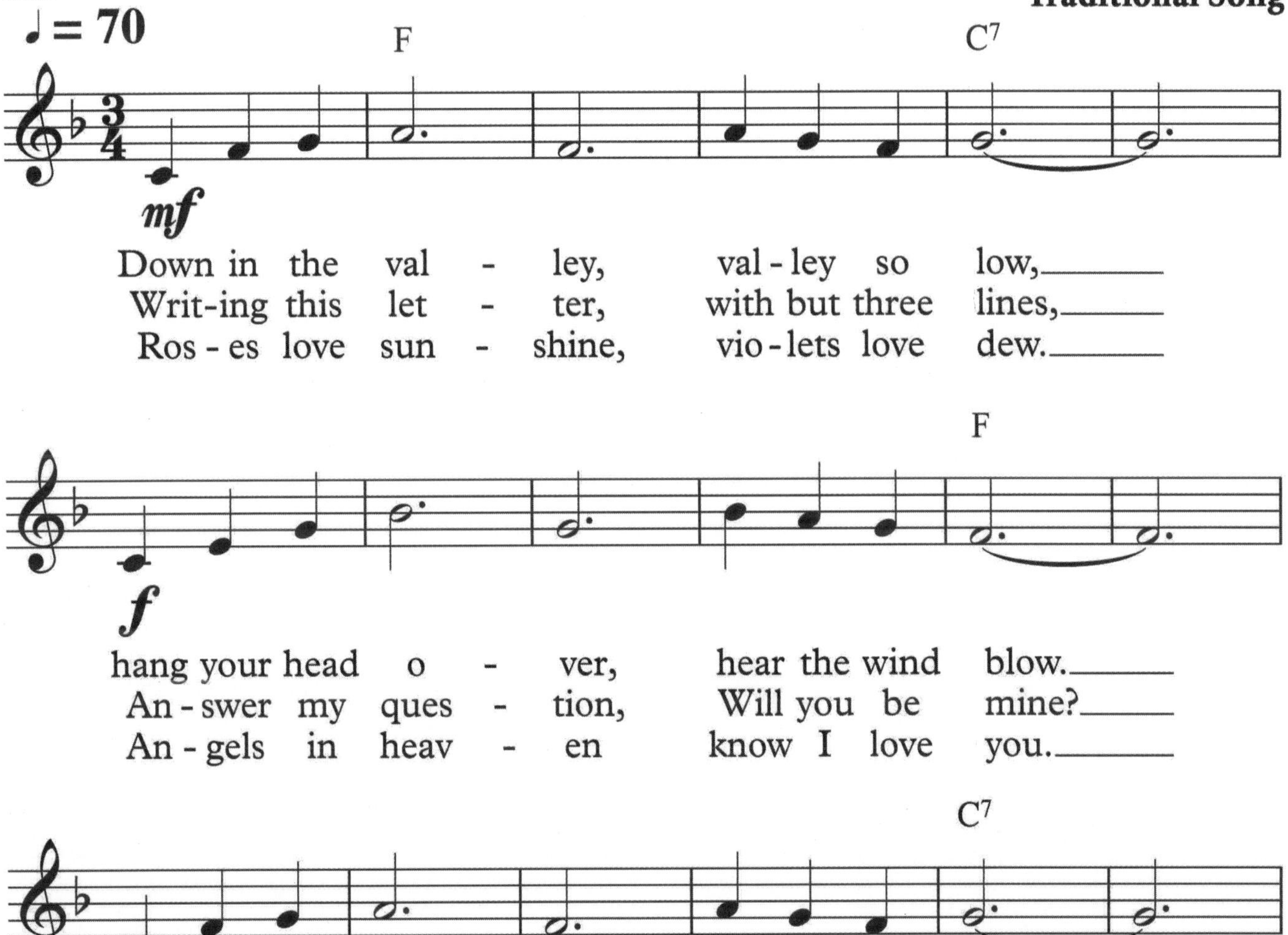

♩ = 70
F
C7
mf
Down in the val - ley, val - ley so low,
Writ-ing this let - ter, with but three lines,
Ros - es love sun - shine, vio - lets love dew.
F
f
hang your head o - ver, hear the wind blow.
An - swer my ques - tion, Will you be mine?
An - gels in heav - en know I love you.
C7
p
Hear the wind blow, dear, hear the wind blow,
Will you be mine, dear, will you be mine?
Know I love you, dear, know I love you.
F
mf
Hang your head o - ver, hear the wind blow.
An - swer my ques - tion, Will you be mine?
An - gels in heav - en know I love you.

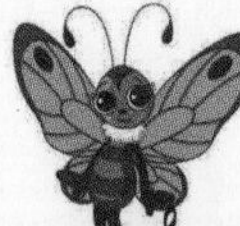

- Practice singing “Down In The Valley,” with beautiful intonation and expression.
- Practice singing with a metronome.
- Pay attention to the details of pitch and dynamics.

Let's Have Fun Learning Piano

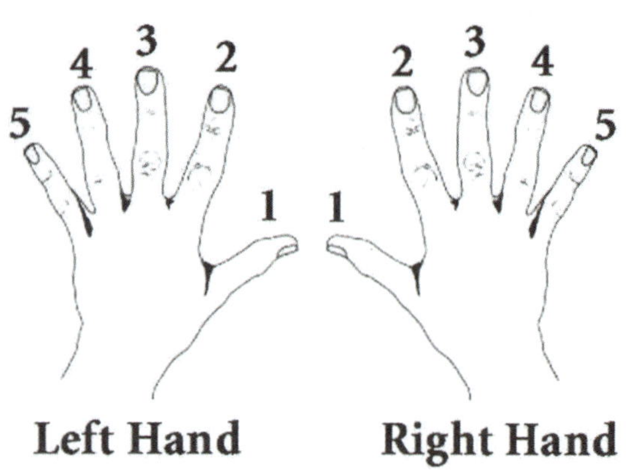

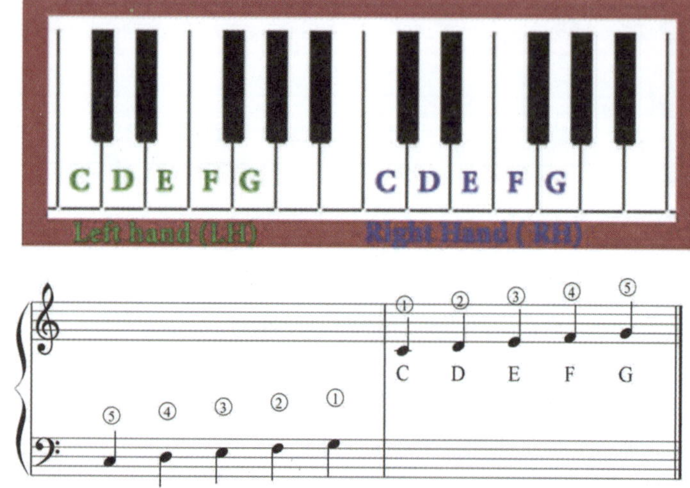

Beautiful Day

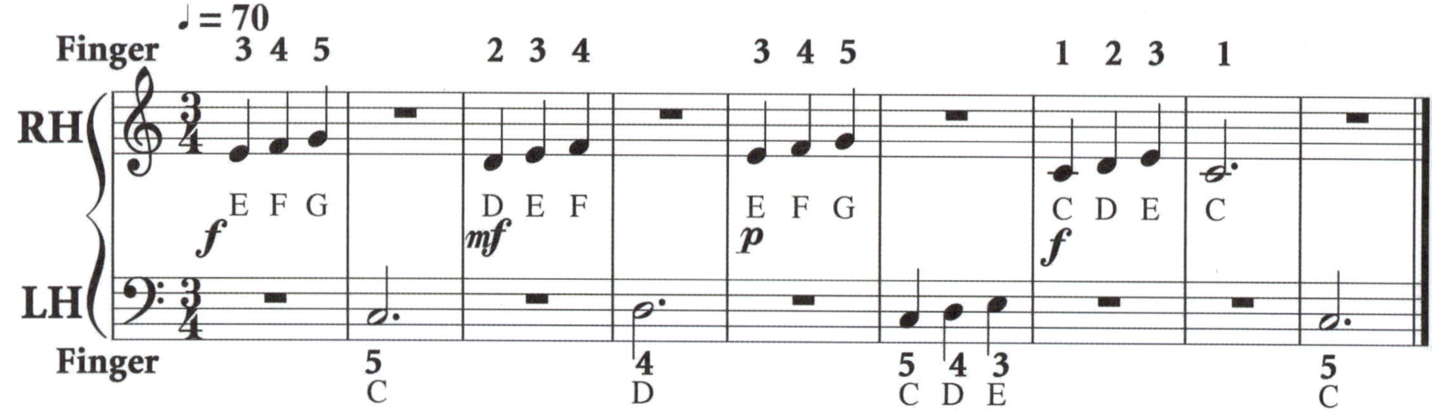

• Balance your right and left hand on all five fingertips.

• Begin by playing right-hand fingers 3, 4, 5, followed by left-hand finger 5. Continue playing right-hand fingers 3, 4, 5, followed by left-hand finger 4, and so on until you finish playing the song.

• With rounded fingers, play the "Beautiful Day."

• Loud passages in the song are always played with heavy pressure on the keys. On the contrary soft passages will be played with less pressure on the keys.

• Say the finger numbers or letters aloud.

Claude Debussy

Claude Debussy was born in 1862 into a poor family in France. At the tender age of 11, he went to the Paris Conservatory to study piano.

Embracing nontraditional tonal structures and scales, Claude Debussy is one of the most highly regarded composers of the late 19th and early 20th centuries. He is seen as the founder of musical impressionism. His contribution to the art of music won him the status of Chevalier of the "Legion of Honour" in 1903.

Claude Debussy earned a scholarship to the Académie des Beaux-Arts after winning the Prix de Rome in 1884 with his composition "The Prodigal Son" on a libretto by Édouard Guinan. He was expected to remain at the Villa Médicis, the French Academy in Rome, for four years as part of the terms and conditions.

On January 28, 1885, he relocated to Rome. He considered the atmosphere at Villa Médicis to be too suffocating for composition at first. However, over time, he started making friends and began composing new pieces.

He also started studying Richard Wagner's music, especially his opera *Tristan und Isolde.* He quickly became a fan of Wagner's music, but he did not like his extroverted emotionalism.

Debussy left Rome for good on March 2, 1887, and returned to Paris.

Back in Paris, he started living in his parents' house, where he enjoyed his brother Emmanuel's company.

Debussy died in March 1918, during the last German offensive of World War I, when Paris was bombarded by airships and long-range weapons.

Debussy at the Villa Medici in Rome, 1885, at center in the white jacket

Selected Works by Claude Debussy

Piano Works

Suite Bergamasque - 1890
First Book of Preludes - 1910
Second Book of Preludes - 1913
Etudes - 1915

Orchestral Works

Nocturnes - 1899
La Mer - 1905
Images - 1912

Coloring Time...Fun...Fun

Claude Debussy

Audio F70

While coloring, you may listen to *Suite Bergamasque,* composed by Claude Debussy.

Claude Debussy Quiz

1. Debussy was born on August 22, 1862 in ____________________.
a) Germany
b) France
c) Italy
d) United States of America

2. Which of the following terms (borrowed from art) is often used to describe Debussy's music?
a) Fauvist
b) Impressionist
c) Cubist
d) Surrealist

3. In 1884, Claude Debussy won the Prix de Rome with his composition _______________.
a) *Claire de Lune*
b) *Fur Elise*
c) *The Prodigal Son*

4. His marvelous contribution to the art of music won him the status of Chevalier of the "Legion of Honor" in 1903.
a) True
b) False

Form

The suite is an important instrumental form of Baroque music. It consists of a number of pieces, each of which has a dance-like character and is all written in the same tone.
Suites are ordered sets of instrumental or orchestral pieces usually performed in a concert setting. (Some dance suites by Bach are called partitas, although this term is also used for other collections of musical pieces).

A dance suite typically consists of four movements (described below), in addition to an overture at the beginning. In the 17th century, famous composers such as Handel and Bach wrote suites. The suites were collections of dances: usually an allemande, a courante, a sarabande, and a gigue. Sometimes other dances were included as well, minuet, gavotte, passepied, or bourree. The first movement, sometimes, was an introduction, not a dance movement. It may have been called a prelude or even overture. A few of Bach's suites were called Partitas.

A Baroque suite is a series of Baroque dances that is often accompanied by a prelude. All parts are in the same key but with different tempos and time signatures. The suite is also known as a partita and a sonata.

Baroque Orchestral Suite

George Frideric Handel - Water Music

- Lively rhythms and catchy melodies
- Opens with French overture
- Bouree - Hornpipe
  - English country dance in lively triple meter
  - A-B-A form
- Terraced dynamics

Basic Suite Form

Allemande	Courante	Sarabande	Gigue
Slow Quadruple meter	Fast Duple or Triple meter	Slow Triple meter	Very Fast Duple or Triple meter

Movements of the Baroque Suite

Overture

The Baroque suite often began with a French overture ("Ouverture" in French), which was followed by a succession of dances, principally the following four: Allemande, Courante, Sarabande, and Gigue.

The overture was first found in Jean-Baptiste Lully's overtures from the early Baroque era. Other famous overtures are in some of Bach's suites (Orchestral Suites, Partita in D major, etc.). It was also used as an opening to operas and oratorios by Handel (including his very famous *Messiah*).

 Audio F72 George Frideric Handel *Messiah-Overture*

Allemande

The first dance of an instrumental suite, the allemande, was a popular dance with origins dating back to the German Renaissance era. The allemande was played at a moderate tempo and could start on any beat of the bar.

Defining features:

- Moderate tempo
- Usually in 4/4
- Serious sound and mood

Listening example:

J. S. Bach's *Allemande from Cello Suite no.1 in G major (BWV 1007)*

2. Allemande

Suite per violoncello n° 1 Johann Sebastian BACH

Courante

The courante is the second dance in a Baroque dance suite and originated in the late Renaissance in France and Italy. Courante literally means "running," and was danced with fast, "running" steps.

Audio F74 'Courante' from Cello Suite no.1

Defining features:

- Usually in 3/2 or 3/4
- Lively and fast
- A sweet character

Listening example:

J. S. Bach's *Courante from Cello Suite no.1 in G major (BWV 1007)*

Sarabande

The Sarabande is a dance in triple meter, is a dance that was popular in Baroque music. The Sarabande was a slow, stately dance with three beats in a bar (3/4 time or Simple Triple).

Defining features:

- Usually in 3/4
- Very slow
- Has a halting sound due to emphasis on the second beat

Listening example:

J. S. Bach's *Sarabande from Cello Suite no.1 in G major (BWV 1007)*

Sarabande

Suite per violoncello n° 1

BWV 1007

Johann Sebastian BACH

Gigue

Gigue is an upbeat and lively Baroque dance in compound meter, typically the concluding movement of an instrumental suite and the fourth of its basic dance types. It can begin from any beat of the bar and is easily recognizable through its characteristic rhythmic feel. Gigue originated from the British Isles.

Defining features:

- Compound time (like 3/8 or 6/8)
- Lively and Fast
- Contrapuntal texture

Listening example:

J. S. Bach's *Gigue from Cello Suite no.1 in G major (BWV 1007)*

Gigue

Optional extra dances

Here are various dances that might be found sandwiched between the 3rd and 4th dance movement (sarabande and gigue):

Gavotte
Bourree
Minuet
Passepied
Rigaudon

Prelude

Preludes are short musical pieces with an undefined structure. Preludes were originally conceived as introductory pieces, either to another more complex piece, to a suite of movements, or to a large-scale work. The early preludes, which were typically written for the keyboard, were extremely improvisatory in nature.

Prelude gradually developed into a stand-alone concert piece, and Johann Sebastian Bach composed the first key-organized sets of preludes. Many composers will follow suit in the years that followed. J.S. Bach gave each prelude its own distinct character; some are akin to arias, others to dance forms, toccatas, or inventions.

Preludes of Frédéric Chopin and Claude Debussy are brief, self-contained pieces that vary widely in character but often explore a particular mood. Prelude in its' true nature is a keyboard form, but it does occur in orchestral music, for example, as an introduction to an act of an opera or in a more conceptual mode, like Debussy's famous tone-poem for chamber orchestra, *Prelude to the Afternoon of a Faun.* You may listen to some famous examples of a prelude.

- Frederic Chopin, *Prelude Op. 28, No. 4 in E Minor*
- Johann Sebastian Bach, *Prelude in C major from The Well Tempered Clavier, Book One*

Audio F77

Audio F78

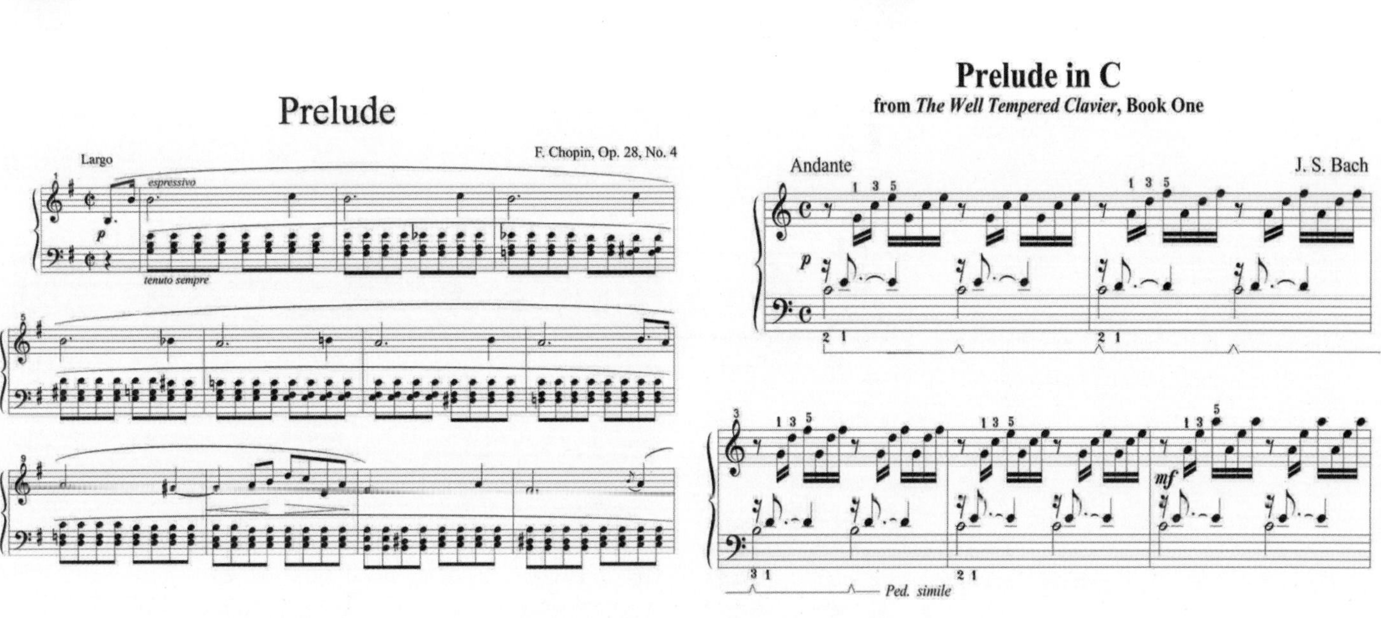

Treble Clef Notes

Write the following words in musical notes on the treble staff.

FADE

AGED

FACE

BEEF

CAGE

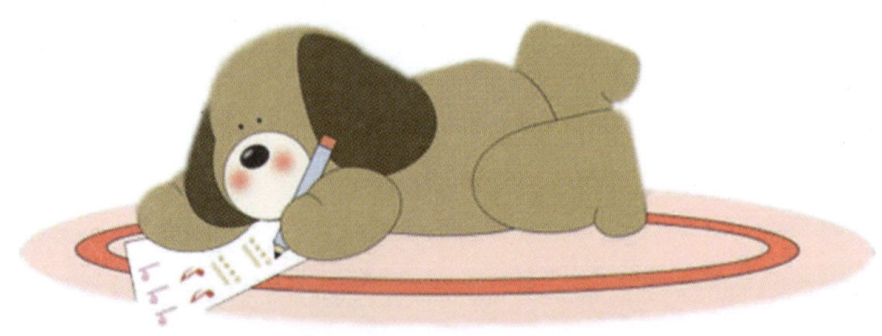

Fun...Fun...Fun... Rhythm Practice

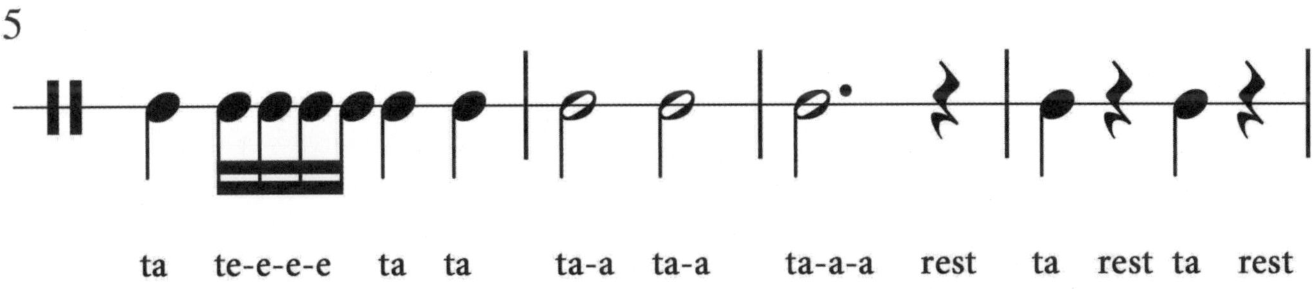

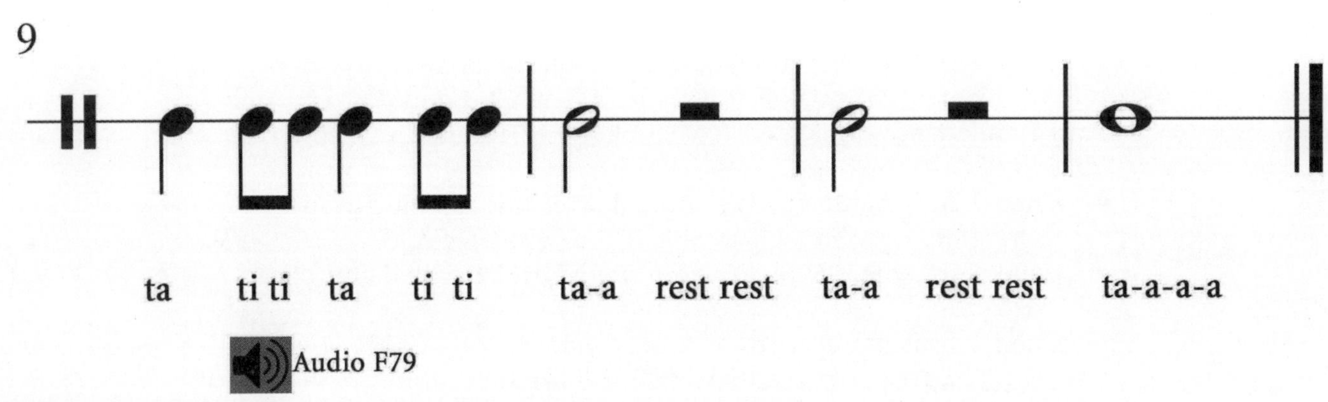

- Write in the beat below each musical note, and the rest indicated.
- Clap the rhythm. Repeat if necessary.
- Listen, tune, and blend your voice with other voices around you.
- Take a full, expanded rib cage breath before each repetition.
- Notice the eighth and sixteenth note, alongside the rests.
- Accuracy is more important than speed, hence take it slow while practicing.
- Practice this rhythm exercise with a metronome.

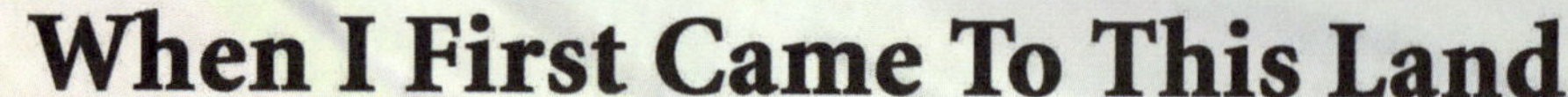

When I First Came To This Land

Audio F80

Traditional Song

1. When I first came to this land, I was not a wealthy man.
Then I got myself a shack, I did what I could.
And I called my shack, "Break my back."

Refrain
For the land was sweet and good, I did what I could.

2. When I first came to this land, I was not a wealthy man.
Then I got myself a cow, I did what I could.
And I called my cow, "No Milk Now,"
and I called my shack, "Break My Back" Refrain

3. When I first came to this land, I was not a wealthy man.
Then I got myself a duck, I did what I could.
And I called my duck, "Out of Luck," and I called my cow...

4. When I first came to this land, I was not a wealthy man.
Then I got myself a wife, I did what I could.
And I called my wife, "Run for Your Life," and I called my duck...

5. When I first came to this land, I was not a wealthy man.
Then I got myself a son, I did what I could.
And I called my son, "Your Work's Done," and I called my wife...

- Begin by singing the song all the way through, then sing a two-measure phrase at a time, with the students echoing short phrases. Then echo the four-measure phrase and finally the entire song.
- Have students discover the pitches of the song.
- Sing the entire song reinforcing the direction of the melody with your hand.
- Identify and understand the F sharp and C sharp.
- Identify the same, different, and similar melodic patterns.
- Did you notice the time signature?

Igor Stravinsky

Igor Fedorovich Stravinsky was born in Oranienbaum near St. Petersburg, Russia, on June 17, 1882. Although his father was a star singer at the Imperial Opera, he expected his son to become a bureaucrat. Igor completed his law studies before he made the decision to become a musician. By this time, he was already a good pianist, an enthusiastic reader of avant-garde (non-traditional) scores from France and Germany, and occasional professional accompanist (someone who plays along with a singer), and a connoisseur (expert) of Italian, French, and Russian opera.

Stephan Mitusov was a close friend of Stravinsky, the stepson of a prince. Mitusov translated poems of the French poet Paul Verlaine (1884–1896) that Stravinsky set to music in 1910 and arranged the libretto (text that accompanies a musical work) of Stravinsky's opera *The Nightingale*.

One of Stravinsky's colleagues at the university was Vladimir Rimsky-Korsakov, the son of renowned composer Nikolai Rimsky-Korsakov (1844–1908). Stravinsky became a student to the elder Rimsky-Korsakov. He did not enroll himself at the Conservatory but worked privately at his home.

In order to learn the most advanced skills from Rimsky-Korsakov, Stravinsky hid his independent taste, confident that he could exercise it later. His *Symphony in E-flat* (1905–1907), *Pastorale* (1907), and *Fireworks* (1908) are worthy demonstrations of his diverse taste. Stravinsky wrote a funeral dirge (a dark, moody piece) for Rimsky-Korsakov, which he later recalled as one of the best of his early compositions. It was not published, and the manuscript was lost.

Coloring Time...Fun...Fun

Igor Stravinsky

Audio F81

While coloring, you may listen to *Fireworks,* composed by Igor Stravinsky.

Igor Stravinsky Quiz

1. Igor Fedorovich Stravinsky was born in ________________.
a) Russia
b) Italy
c) Germany
d) France

2. Igor finished a university law course before he made the decision to become a musician.
a) True
b) False

3. Stravinsky became an apprentice to ________________________.
a) Franz Schubert
b) Antonio Vivaldi
c) Rimsky-Korsakov

4. Igor Stravinsky was one of the most influential composers of the ________________.
a) Baroque Era
b) 20th century
c) Classical Era

Harmony/Texture

Harmony in music is when you hear or play two or more notes at the same time. In Western music, most harmony is based on chords. Harmony can refer to the arrangement of musical notes in a chord and the overall chord structure of a piece of music. In music theory, harmony refers to building chords, chord qualities, and chord progressions.

Down By The Station

Audio F82

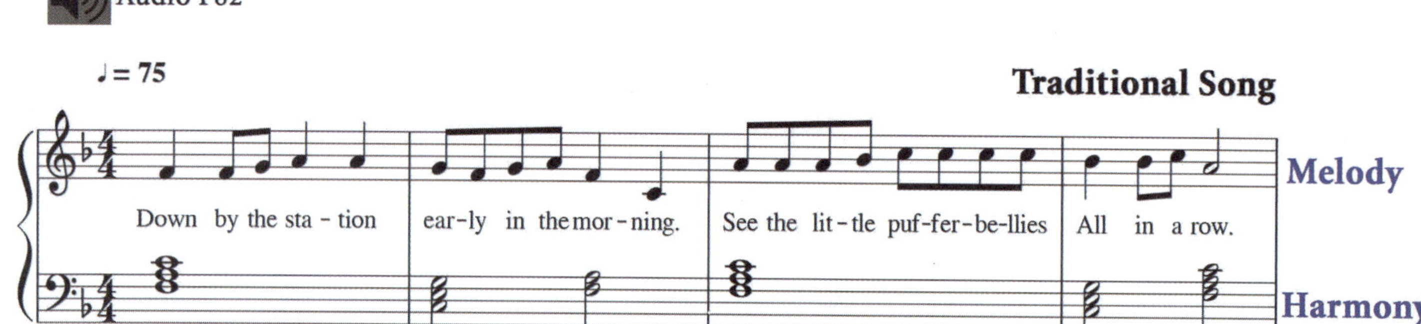

The origins of the "harmony" word come from the Greek word Harmonia, meaning agreement. Sometimes harmony may not be particularly "harmonious"; it may be quite dissonant.

Harmony is a combination of simultaneously sounded notes to produce chords having a pleasing effect, or scarry effect, or sad effect, etc.

The most used chords in music will use at least three notes. For example, the chord of C is created by playing the notes of C, E, and G together. The chord of A minor is created by playing A, C, and E together.

Harmony is often said to refer to the "vertical" aspect of music, distinguished from the melodic line, or the "horizontal" aspect.

Close position C major triad

Audio F83

Open position C major triad.

Audio F84

Texture deals with how various musical sounds and melodic lines blend with each other. It is the interrelationship of voices and instruments. While hearing texture in music, one must inquire how many melodies are being played and how are they related to each other? The three textures in music are:

Monophonic
Polyphonic
Homophonic

Monophonic

Monophony is one main melody (mono=one, phony=sound). A single-line melody is unaccompanied and unadorned. Many times the monophonic texture is not enough information to capture the audience's attention. The exceptions are vocal chants such as plainsong and certain pieces sung a cappella such as "Amazing Grace."

Polyphonic

Polyphony is a type of musical texture consisting of two or more melodies of equal importance played or sung simultaneously. Polyphonic music can also be called polyphony, contrapuntal, or counterpoint music. If more than one independent melody is occurring at the same time, the music is polyphonic.

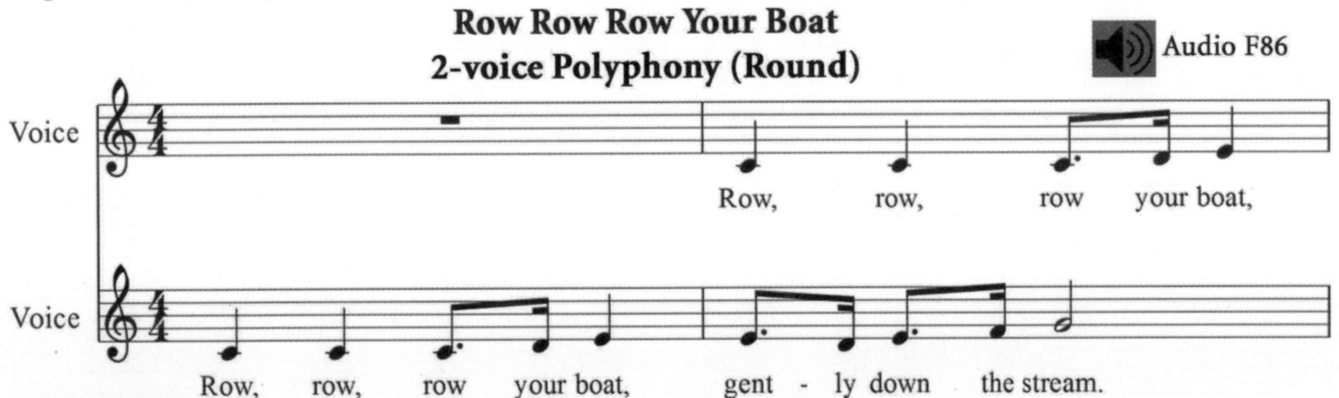

Homophonic

Homophony is a musical texture in which one melody predominates while the other parts play either single notes or an elaborate accompaniment. An example can be found in Haydn's Symphony No. 94, mvt 2 (nicknamed "Surprise"), the violins bring the melody, and the lower strings support it with a bass line and chords.

Homophonic music is also sometimes called chordal music.

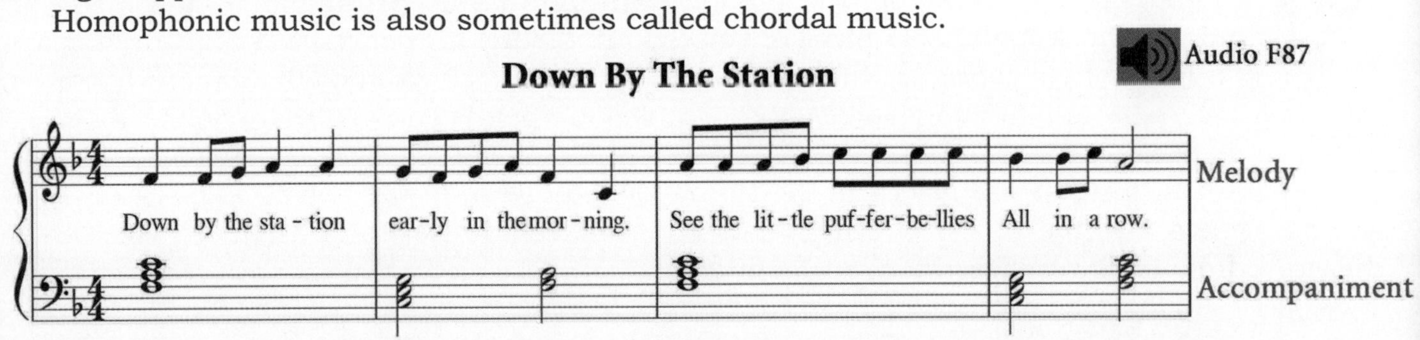

Row, Row, Row, Your Boat
2-voice Polyphony (Round)

Voice
Row, row, row your boat,

Voice
Row, row, row your boat, gent - ly down the stream.

3
Vo.
gent - ly down the stream.

Vo.
Mer - ri - ly mer - ri - ly mer - ri - ly mer - ri - ly

4
Vo.
Mer - ri - ly mer - ri - ly mer - ri - ly mer - ri - ly life is but a dream!

Vo.
life is but a dream!

Let us sing "Row, Row, Row, Your Boat" as a "round." After the 1st voice begins, the 2nd voice comes in. A "round" is a polyphonic vocal composition in which three or four voices follow each other around in a perpetual canon at the unison or octave. A canon is a piece of voices (or instrumental parts) that play or sing the same song starting at different times. A round is a form of the canon; however, the difference here is that every voice can begin again when it ends so that the piece can go round and round.

You will continue to add voices to the round to add layers to the polyphonic texture. Try adding a third and fourth voice. Simply postpone the entry of each subsequent voice until the preceding voice reaches the word "gently."

Counter-melody

In a piece of music, a counter-melody is a melody that complements the main theme. It can even stand on its own while subordinate. Here are some suggestions that I have collected for writing a counter-melody:

• Counter means the reverse. It doesn't mean otherwise.

• The same scale can be used for the counter-melody and the melody (with harmony).

• The counter-melody sounds fine when performed alone.

• The counter-melody, too, sounds fine when performed with the main melody.

• A counter-melody with the main melody or harmony does not interfere. A different octave, a different sounding instrument, a different beat, or both of these methods may be used.

• The counter-melody is active while the main melody rests and vice-versa. A counter-melody is essentially a secondary melody designed to "counter" the main melody. To stick out throughout the texture, it usually assumes a particular pattern and contour (shape) than the primary melody. Sing this counter-melody sample:

Who Has Seen the Wind?

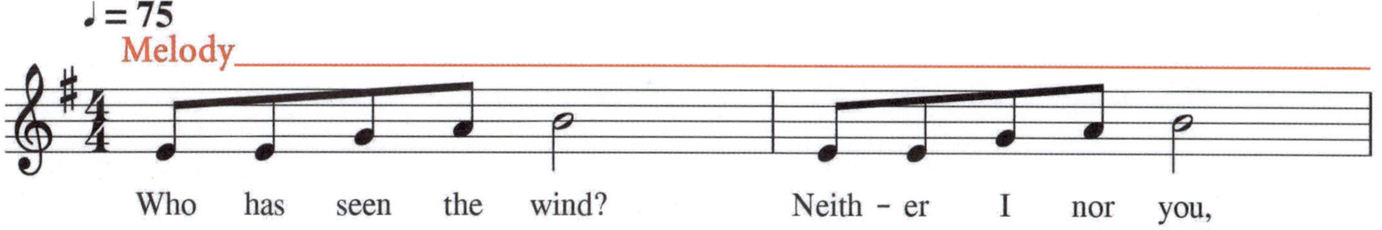

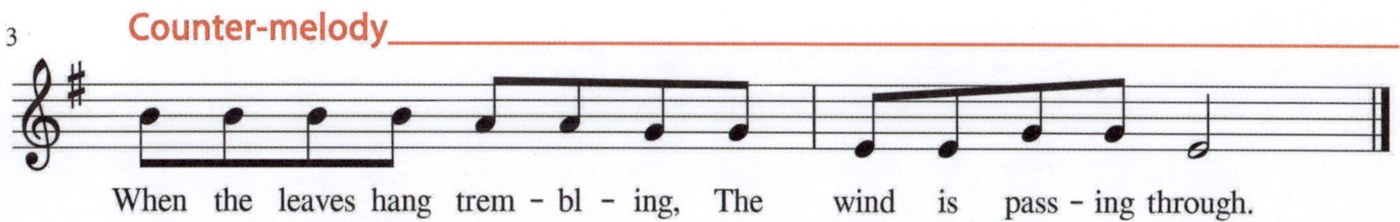

1. Who has seen the wind?
Neither I nor you.
When the leaves hang trembling,
The wind is passing through.

2. Who has seen the wind?
Neither you nor I;
But when the trees bow down their heads
The wind is passing by.

Partner Song

There are two specific meanings of the word "partner song," also named "quodlibet,":

1) Two or more completely independent songs that appear to have the same harmonic arrangement by chance and may thus be performed together at the same time.

2) A song composed deliberately with multiple independent lines that all harmonize to create an interlocking "partnership" with each other.

The harmonies and joys of counterpoint or polyphony are based on rounds and partner songs: that is, music made up of independent lines moving alongside each other and constantly combining in various ways, producing new turns, fascinating perspectives, and tempting bridges.

Audio F90

My Home's in Montana

Traditional Song

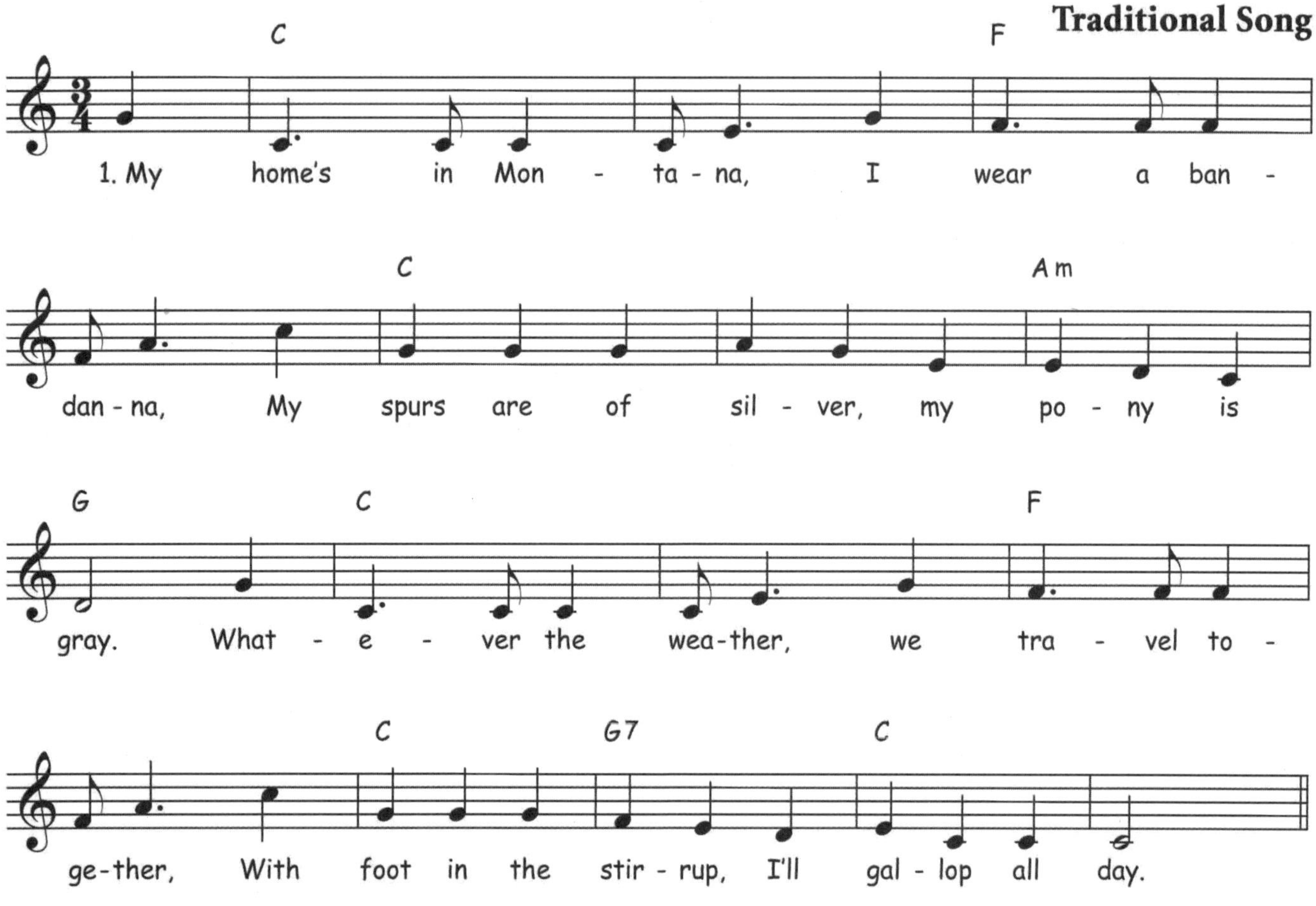

C F
1. My home's in Mon - ta - na, I wear a ban -

C Am
dan - na, My spurs are of sil - ver, my po - ny is

G C F
gray. What - e - ver the wea-ther, we tra - vel to -

C G7 C
ge-ther, With foot in the stir - rup, I'll gal - lop all day.

Partner songs are two individual melodies that fit together in such a way that they sound good when performed together. These melodies are performed as independent musical voices; harmony is created when two or more melodic voices are performed at the same time. In all partner songs, each performer should sing their lines independently before all parts are sung simultaneously.

Ostinato

Ostinato, (Italian: "obstinate") plural Ostinatos, or Ostinati, in music, a short melodic phrase repeated throughout a composition, sometimes slightly varied or transposed to a different pitch. A rhythmic ostinato is a short, repeated, continuously rhythmic pattern.

Can you find other short ostinato melodies or rhythms in this song?

Unison

Unison derives from the Latin root words uni, which means "one," and sonous, which means "sound." So, unison simply means one sound, and that sense is preserved in music.

Unison happens when the same pitch or the same octaves are performed or sung by two or more individuals. You may have encountered unison talking outside of music, such as when your class recites something together or unison movement, or when a group performs a dance routine.

In the case of music composed for several instruments, when two (or more) persons perform precisely the same note, exactly the same way, on two separate instruments, a perfect harmonic unison takes place.

In this notation, see an example of unison, which illustrates the same notes for both parts.

Both the upper and lower staves show the same notes; they are in unison.

Descant

A descant is an extra vocal component, an independent treble melody usually sung or played above the basic melody in the song. A descant sang at a higher pitch than the melody, which is used in many church hymns.

The I, IV, and V Chords

In each major key, the chords I, IV, and V are the three most commonly used chords. On the first note of the key, Chord I is constructed. Chord IV is built on the key's fourth tone, and chord V is built on the key's fifth note. The key of C major is made up of the following notes: C, D, E, F, G, A, and B.

C is the first note, F is the fourth note, and G is the sixth. The C major triad, the F major triad, and the G major triad are the I, IV, and V chords in the key of C. In a nutshell, we would clearly say, 'C, F, and G are the chords.'

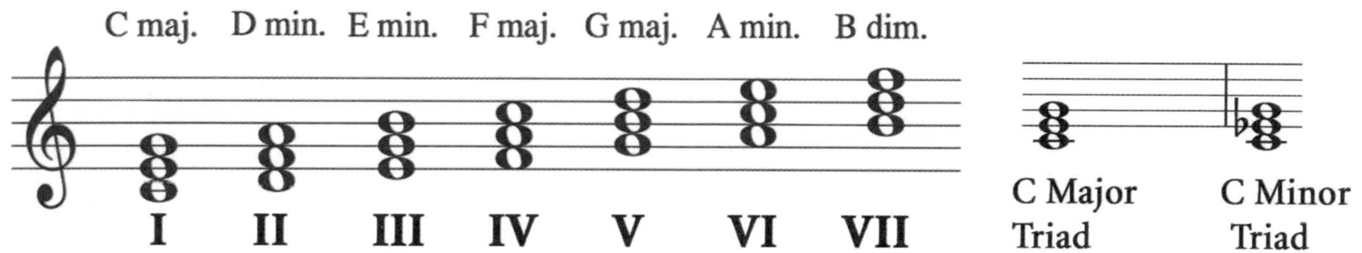

Start with a single pitch, the root, and add a major third (four half steps) note above to create a major triad. Then, add a minor third note above that (three half-steps). For instance, the notes C, E, and G comprise a C major triad.

The opposite order of intervals is used to construct a minor triad: a minor third interval is above the root, and a major third "stacks" on top to complete the triad. So, the notes are C, E♭, and G in the C minor triad.

Note that the root note and the top note are still a perfect fifth (seven half-steps) apart, in both major and minor triads. Whether the triad is major or minor, all depends on the middle pitch.

Singing Major and Minor Triads

A triad is a set of three notes related by thirds. In the illustration below, each one of the note groupings is a triad. Note that each one is two-thirds of a stack. The first group is a triad formed on the C note. Three notes C, E, and G, are used in the triad (C to E is a third, and E to G is a third-a stack of two-thirds). A triad based on "D," etc., is the next group of notes. The notes move from line to line or space to space on the staff. A major triad consists of Do, Mi, Sol, the first, third, and fifth notes of a major scale. It's a broken triad if the notes are played one after the other. It is called a solid triad if the notes are played simultaneously.

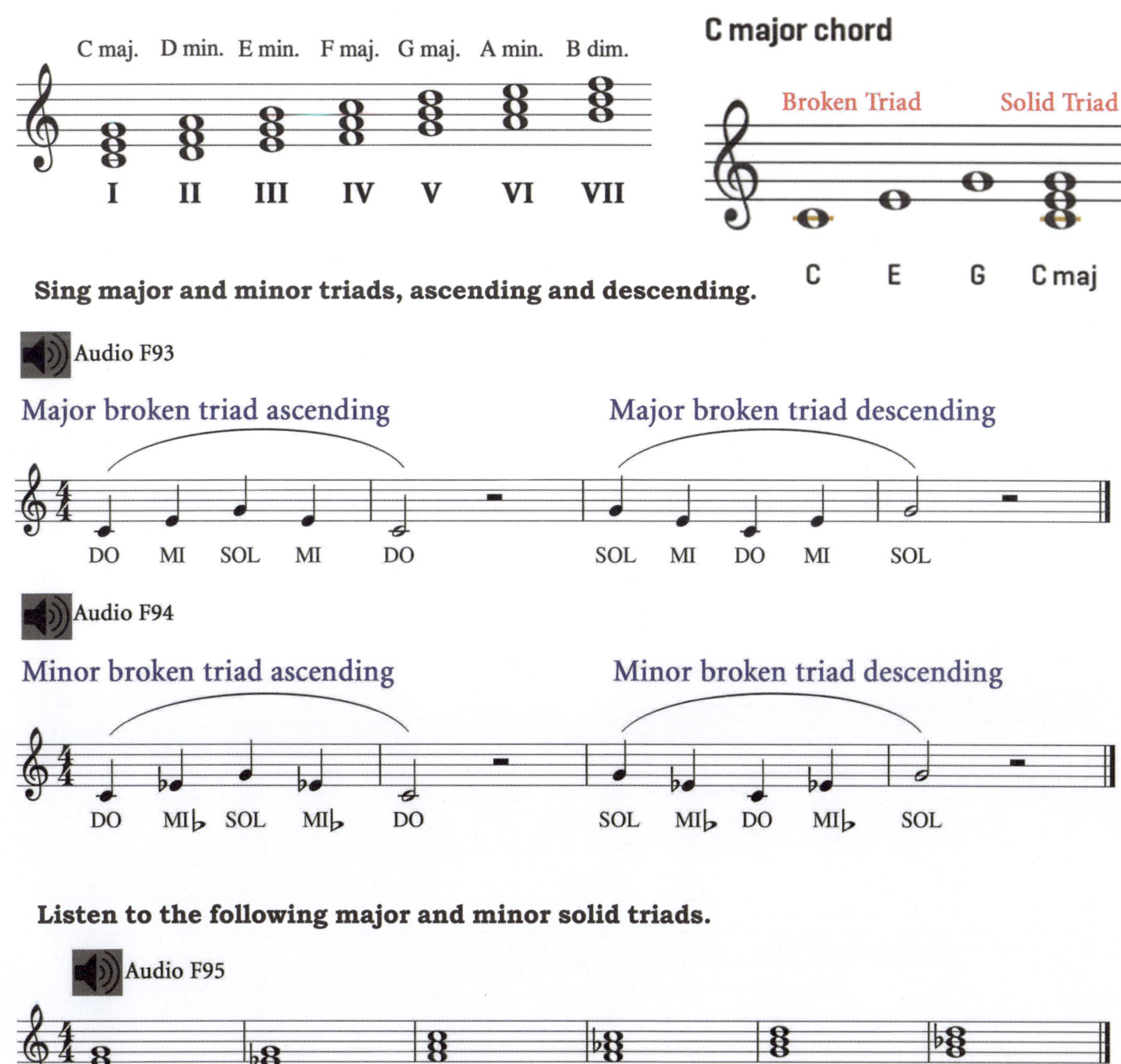

C Major C Minor F Major F Minor G Major G Minor

Did you notice that major chords have brighter, cheerier sound, and minor chords have darker and sadder sound?

Happy Birthday

Audio F96

Traditional Song

- Practice singing the song "Happy Birthday."
- Have students discover song pitches.
- Sing the entire song reinforcing the direction of the melody with your hand.
- Identify and understand the chord changes throughout the song.
- Recognize different and similar melodic patterns.

Audio F97

Solfege

♩ = 75

5

Voice 1

DO MI SOL SOL DO MI FA FA RE

mf *f*

Voice 2

SOL MI SOL DO FA FA RE

p *f*

7

Voice 1

RE DO MI DO MI SOL DO

mf *f*

Voice 2

RE SOL DO SOL MI SOL DO

p *f*

Divide children into two groups. Repeat the melody line and rhythm multiple times. After, sing the solfege exercise as a duet. Observe the right pitch and rhythm of the singing. Sing this solfege exercise applying correct dynamics and tempo.

On this page point out, and circle the dotted half notes, tie notes, and dynamics. Take this slowly and really concentrate on how each note sounds.

In each measure, we have three beats. Sing a bit louder the first solfege syllable of the first beat.

Note! A musical line that creates a definite tune is a melodic line. Unison singing is an example of single melodic lines for songs, whereas round songs/partner songs are examples of multiple melodic lines for songs.

In music, the overall quality of a sound is defined by the texture. It may be heavy or light, thick or thin. The musical texture relies on the number of melodic lines contained in a song. In a piece, the more melodic lines, the thicker the sound. Thicker musical sounds are produced by singing in rounds, duets, partner songs, and incorporating rhythmical accompaniment. How many melodic lines are there for you to see?

Solfege

- Divide children into three groups.
- Repeat the melody line and rhythm multiple times.
- After that, sing the "Solfege Exercise" in two voices with rhythmic accompaniment.
- Accuracy in pitch and rhythm is of utmost importance.
- Practice with a metronome.

Remember!

- More melodic lines, thicker sound.
- Less melodic lines, thinner sound.

Who Has Seen the Wind?

Audio F99

♩ = 75

Round is a musical arrangement in which at least two voices sing (and can proceed to repeat indefinitely) precisely the same melody in unison, except with each voice starting at random points, such that different parts of the melody correspond with different voices, but still match together harmoniously.

Students should be divided into two groups for round singing, “Who Has Seen the Wind?”

Here, the first group starts ahead, while the second group follows after the first phrase. Students can demonstrate the concept of texture in music by singing a two-part round.

Remember!

We have a single melodic line when we sing songs in unison; and multiple melodic lines when we sing in round. A single melodic line produces a thin sound and multiple melodic lines produce thick sounds.

Antonin Dvorak

Antonin Dvorak (full name Antonin Leopold Dvorak) was born on September 8, 1841, as the first of nine children to Anna and Frantisek Dvorak. He was born in the village of Nelahozeves, near Prague, where his father was a butcher. Although his early circumstances were relatively humble, he learned violin, viola, piano, and organ at school. Young Dvorak was clearly more interested in music composition and was destined for a great career in music. He later studied in Prague and played viola in the Provisional Theatre Orchestra for a few years. This gave him the much-needed practical experience of not only performing but also of orchestral arrangements. This orchestra's chief conductor was none other than Bedrich Smetana. Smetana was the founding father of his country's nationalist school of music, and Dvorak would follow in his footsteps for the rest of his life out of respect.

Another notable composer who influenced Dvorak was Richard Wagner. Dvorak played in a concert of Wagner excerpts conducted by the composer himself, and this experience had a noticeable impact on the direction that Dvorak was to take.

Between 1892 and 1895 he spent some time in the United States of America as director of the new National Conservatory, a period that brought compositions which combined both American and Bohemian influence.

the room where Antonin Dvorak was born

Dvorak composed nine symphonies, the most famous of which is Symphony No. 9, "From the New World," published in 1893 and premiered in New York the same year. This "New World" Symphony was inspired by a Czech version of Longfellow's poem "Hiawatha."

Dvorak's works for solo instrument and orchestra include a significant cello concerto, a violin concerto, and a much less well-known piano concerto. The *Romance* for solo violin and orchestra and *Silent Woods* for solo cello and orchestra are both intriguing and appealing additions to the solo repertoire for both instruments.

Dvorak was one of the several composers from the Romantic era who let his cultural roots shine through his music. He died in 1904, shortly after the premiere of his final opera, *Armida*.

Coloring Time...Fun...Fun

Antonin Dvorak

Audio F100

While coloring, you may listen to *Symphony No. 9* “From the New World,” composed by Antonin Dvorak.

Antonin Dvorak Quiz

1. Antonin Dvorak was born in ________________.
a) Rome
b) Paris
c) Prague
d) New York

2. Dvorak held the position of ____________________ while he was in the United States?
a) Director of the National Conservatory
b) Director of the Philharmonic Orchestra
c) Director of the Chicago Symphony Orchestra

3. Dvorak wrote nine symphonies, of which the best known is the *Symphony No 9*, "From the New World," written in 1893 and first performed in New York in the same year.
a) True
b) False

4. Antonin Dvorak was one of the most influential composers of the ___________________.
a) Baroque Era
b) 20th-century
c) Classical Era
d) Romantic Era

Let's compose a rhythm exercise

3

5

7

- Using the whole note/rest, half note/rest, quarter note/rest, eighth note/rest, and sixteenth note/rest to compose seven rhythm measures.
- In a 4/4 time signature, the rhythm exercise would be composed, and thus any measure must have four beats.
- Clap, tap, or chant the rhythm.
- Have fun composing this rhythm exercise.

Classical Music Styles

Music From Various Historical Periods

Medieval (500-1400)

This period is broken down into three eras: Early Medieval music (before 1150), High Medieval music (1150-1300), and Late Medieval music (1300-1400). The most famous composition of all three periods was the Gregorian chant, an unaccompanied sacred song of the Roman Catholic Church. Other popular music included Organum, Cantigas de Santa Maria, and Troubadour. Composers like German Hildegard von Bingen and French Guillaume de Machaut used pan flutes, modern recorders, string instruments, jaw harps, and early versions of the organ, fiddle, and trombone.

The Style of Middle Ages Music

Music from the Early Middle Ages was played first in unison. Usually, the notes were of the same duration and were sung or performed in C Key. Harmony was introduced gradually. By the 12th century, a musical notation method was developed, which indicated the length of each note along with its pitch.

Audio F101, F102

- *Messe de Nostre Dame* by Guillaume de Machaut
- *Epiphany*- Gregorian Chant

Renaissance Classical (1400-1600)

There was the increased importance of individualism in the cultural movements of the Renaissance Period, which was often expressed in classical music. Like the Gregorian chant, sacred church music becomes more vocal, tapping into human feelings. As new instruments found their way, the instrumental skills of musicians grew greatly and those from the Medieval period were also dramatically enhanced. A popular, unifying musical language, especially the polyphonic style of the Franco-Flemish School, arose from this changing society.

The innovation of the Gutenberg press made music and musical theory distribution available on a mass scale.

The propagation of chansons, motets, and masses throughout Europe culminated with the unification into the flowing form of polyphonic practice, resulting in the works of composers such as Palestrina, Lassus, Victoria, and William Byrd in the second half of the sixteenth century.

Audio F103 • *Gregorianos* by Giovanni Pierluigi da Palestrina

Classical Music Styles

Baroque (1600-1745)

In sculpture, painting, design, writing, dance, theatre, and music, the Baroque period is also thought of as an era of artistic style that used dramatic motion, easily interpreted detail to create suspense, excitement, exuberance, and grandeur. The style originated in Rome, Italy, about 1600, and spread to much of Europe.

During this time, composers further explored the capacity to convey human emotions through highly ornate and colorful compositions.

Orchestras and opera have since grown from undefined ensembles of chamber music to unique performances of wide crowds. The most prominent artists of the Baroque period were the German composers Johann Sebastian Bach, George Frideric Handel, Johann Pachelbel, and the Italian composer Antonio Vivaldi.

It was during the early part of the seventeenth century that a community of composers first developed the genre of opera in Florence, Italy, and Claudio Monteverdi wrote the earliest operatic masterpieces. In the works of the Venetian composer Antonio Vivaldi and the Harpsichord, the instrumental concerto became a hallmark of the Baroque period and finding its best exponent. Dances were formalized into musical suites, and nearly all composers of the period wrote them. But during this period, vocal and choral music also reigned supreme and resulted in the operas and oratorios of George Frideric Handel, a German-born composer.

- *The Four Seasons Concert-Winter* by Antonio Vivaldi
- *Messiah* by George Frideric Handel

Classical (1750-1820)

The Classical period saw the invention of the sonatas, minuets, and concertos, and some of the most incredible symphonies ever written and certainly never before heard in prior periods. It was an expansive and glorious time for making new music.

Ludwig van Beethoven (1770-1827) is likely to remain the most known composers of this period; however, the creative genius of Wolfgang Amadeus Mozart (1756-1791) and their contributions to music make for a worthy argument as to who was more influential.

With the masterful symphonies, sonatas, and string quartets by the Viennese school's three great composers: Franz Joseph Haydn, Wolfgang Amadeus Mozart, and Ludwig van Beethoven, the Classical era achieved its glorious pinnacle. Composers started abandoning the complex polyphony of the Baroque period and considered more homophonic styles. In Baroque music, the ornate melodies commonly found give way to measured and regularly phased tunes. In this musical era, as the quality of instruments improves, an enhancement in dynamic range (volume) occurs. In the notation of their scores, composers specify these complexities in a manner that did not happen in earlier music.

- *Symphony No. 40* by Wolfgang Amadeus Mozart

Classical Music Styles

Romantic Era (1820 to 1900)

The usage of instrumentation in their settings was increased by composers of the period, integrating new instruments into their works while also expanding the orchestra's overall size. In the works produced during this period, percussion instruments, woodwinds, and brass instruments brought even more, color and feeling. Musical pieces were also expanded and shifted more towards the use of harmony than writing songs, mostly driven by melody. The earliest Romantic composers were all born with a difference of a few years in between. This involve Felix Mendelssohn and Robert Schumann, the great German masters; Frédéric Chopin, the Polish piano poet; the French genius; and Franz Liszt, the Hungarian composer, the most outstanding piano showman in history.

During the Romantic Period, opera as a musical form gained considerable popularity in line with instrumental music developments. As the symphony orchestra, the opera passed into the Romantic Era. In stature and the search for stories steeped in national meaning (in the case of Wagner) or passion, the opera's size rose. In the Romantic Period, several of the finest and best-loved operas were written. The magnificence of Italian composers such as Verdi or Puccini's work has brought us countless unforgettable songs. The operatic works produced by Richard Strauss and Wagner are incredibly magnificent and complex. They broadened the opera's harmonic vocabulary, bringing the tonality to new heights.

 Audio F107 • *Tosca* by Giacomo Puccini

In addition to tonal systems, 20th-century composers such as Arnold Schoenberg pursued rare and unorthodox harmonies. Eastern music intrigued the French composer Claude Debussy, and the whole-tone scale developed a type of music called after the Impressionism trend of French painting. Hungarian composer Béla Bartók followed the still strong Nationalist movement's footsteps and fused the music of Hungarian peasants with twentieth-century forms.

Many composers combined jazz music elements with other music styles such as classical and blues. Music during this time also spoke of nationalistic fervor. Some of the famous composers of this era are George Gershwin ("Rhapsody in Blue"), Aaron Copland ("Rodeo").

 Audio F108 • *Rhapsody In Blue* by George Gershwin

Annie Laurie

Have fun singing this song. You can find more fun songs to learn singing on our website https://mymusicjournal.org/overview/

Consider introducing students to a broad selection of musical instruments. What could your students play? Recorder, harmonica, piano, guitar, ukulele, the list goes on!

Optional to teach! You can teach students to play these songs using a musical instrument that you have in the classroom, for example, a recorder.

Music Theory Review

1. Name the following musical notes.

2. Circle the measure that has a syncopated rhythm.

3. Continue writing dotted notes on the lines or spaces.

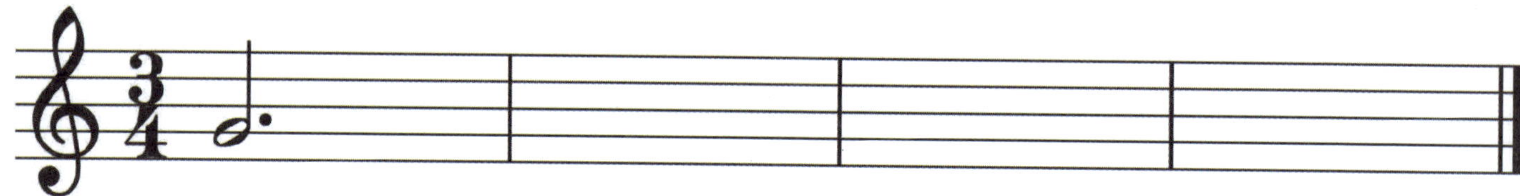

4. How many beats are in a 3/8 time signature?
a) 2 beats
b) 6 beats
c) 3 beats
d) 1 beat

5. In 4/4 time, what type of note gets one beat?
a) a half note
b) an eighth note
c) a quarter note

6. What type of note gets the beat in 2/2 time signature?
a) quarter note
b) sixteenth note
c) half note
d) eighth note

7. Add accidentals to complete each note below. Be sure to carefully place them on the line or in the space in front of the musical note.

G flat E sharp A sharp F flat C natural B flat D sharp E flat A natural D flat C flat E natural

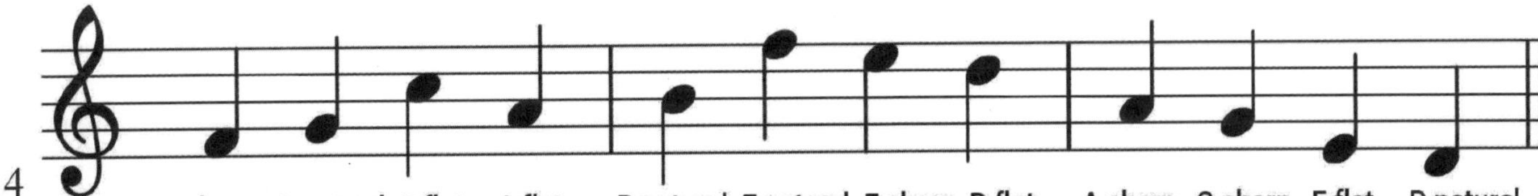

4

F sharp G natural C flat A flat B natural F natural E sharp D flat A sharp G sharp E flat D natural

8. Draw a bass clef at the beginning of the staff and then write each note's letter names.

= = = = = = = =

9. Draw a treble clef at the beginning of the staff, and then draw the indicated notes.

E F G D A B C E F C D

10. What instrument is NOT in the string family?
a) violin
b) viola
c) cello
d) flute

11. A single player is called a ______________________.
a) soloist
b) trio
c) quartet

12. Two performers are known as a ______________________.
a) trio
b) quartet
c) duo
d) orchestra

Glossary of Musical Terms

Absolute music - instrumental music with no intended story (non-programmatic music)

A Cappella - choral music with no instrumental accompaniment

Alto - a low-ranged female voice

Aria - a beautiful manner of solo singing, accompanied by an orchestra, with a steady metrical beat

Atonality - modern harmony, which intentionally avoids a tonal center (has no apparent home key)

Augmentation - lengthening the rhythmic values of a fugal subject

Avant-garde - ("at the forefront") a French term that describes highly experimental modern musical styles

Ballet - (genre) a programmatic theatrical work for dancers and orchestra

Bar - a common term for a musical measure

Baritone - a moderately low male voice; between tenor and bass

Beat - a musical pulse

Binary form - a form comprised of two distinctly opposing sections ("A" vs. "B")

Bitonality - modern music sounding in two different keys simultaneously

Canon - a type of strict imitation created by strict echoing between a melodic "leader" and subsequent "follower(s)"

Cantata - (genre) a composition in several movements, written for chorus, soloist(s), and orchestra; traditionally, these are religious works.

Chamber music - (genre) music performed by a small group of players (one player per part)

Chant - (genre) a monophonic melody sung in a free rhythm (such as the "Gregorian" chant of the Roman Catholic Church)

Consonance - pleasant-sounding harmony

Counter-melody - a secondary melodic idea that accompanies and opposes a main thematic idea

Counterpoint - a complex polyphonic texture combining two or more independent melodies

Duple meter - a basic metrical pattern having two beats per measure

Gregorian chant - (genre) monophonic, non-metered melodies set to Latin sacred texts

Major scale - a family of seven alphabetically ordered pitches within the distance of an octave, following an interval pattern matching the white keys from one "C" to the last "C" of a piano

Mode - a scale or key used in musical composition (major and minor are modes, as are ancient modal scales found in Western music before 1680

Ostinato - a repeated phrase, a short, constantly repeated rhythmic pattern.

Overture - introduction to an opera or other large musical work.

Parody - a composition based on previous work, a common technique used in Medieval and Renaissance music.

Partita - a suite of Baroque dances.

Pastoral - a composition whose style is simple and idyllic, suggestive of rural scenes.

Pentatonic Scale - a musical scale having five notes.

Quadruple meter - a basic metrical pattern having four beats per measure.

Triad - a three-note chord built on alternating scales steps (1-3-5, etc.)

Triple meter - a common meter with three beats per measure

Unison - the simultaneous rendering of a single melodic line by several performers